perfect
chicken

This is a Parragon Publishing book
First published in 2007

Parragon Publishing
Queen Street House
4 Queen Street
Bath BA1 1HE, UK

ISBN 978-1-4054-7366-8

Printed in China

This book uses imperial, metric, and US cup measurements. Follow the same units of measurement throughout; do not mix imperial and metric. All spoon measurements are level, unless otherwise stated: teaspoons are assumed to be 5ml, and tablespoons are assumed to be 15ml. Unless otherwise stated, milk is assumed to be whole, eggs and individual fruits such as bananas are medium, and pepper is freshly ground black pepper.

Recipes using raw or very lightly cooked eggs should be avoided by infants, the elderly, pregnant women, convalescents, and anyone suffering from an illness. Pregnant and breast-feeding women are advised to avoid eating peanuts and peanut products.

perfect
chicken

introduction

Chicken has become one of the most useful and popular meats in nearly all cultures around the world. The reasons for this are many, not least that chickens are relatively quick and easy to raise, and do not require acres of lush grassland! It is worth bearing in mind that a free-range, corn-fed chicken might cost a little more, but it will have a far superior flavor to one that has been intensively farmed.

From a nutritional point of view, chicken is an excellent source of protein, B vitamins, and minerals such as zinc and iron. It is naturally low in fat and has no carbohydrates, making it the dream

food for those who need to keep their weight or cholesterol levels in check. It is very quick and easy to cook, too, so there need be no excuses about not having enough time to produce a healthy, well-balanced meal!

And from a gastronomic point of view? There are so many options that you could serve chicken every day of the week and still not run out of ideas! Chicken can be cooked very simply—roasted, chargrilled, broiled, stir-fried,

or pan-fried—and served with potatoes or rice and salad greens or lightly cooked vegetables. And when you have a little more time to spare, the choices are endless. If you like rice, you can go for a creamy Italian risotto or a saffron-colored Spanish paella; and if you are a pasta lover, you will find some fantastic sauces and might even be inspired to make your own filled pasta shapes, such as tortellini and ravioli. If Mexican food is your thing, there are recipes for fajitas, tacos, and tostadas; and there are Chinese, Thai, and Indian

dishes to satisfy any spice cravings!

Some recipes are specifically for those who are diabetic, or follow a low-fat, low-carb or gluten-free diet—check in the introduction to each chapter for ideas. And whatever your reason for choosing chicken—good health!

soups, appetizers & salads

Chicken and soup seem made for each other, and this chapter has a handful of chicken soups, each with a completely different character, from a light and delicious Clear Soup with Mushrooms & Chicken to a creamy and elegant Chicken & Tarragon Soup. Chicken, Avocado & Chipotle Soup is a Mexican recipe with attitude, and if you are feeling blue, treat yourself to a bowl of Chicken-Noodle Soup, the classic cure-all!

Chicken is a useful ingredient in appetizers. Spanish tapas bars serve it in the form of Crispy Chicken & Ham Croquettes and Chicken in Lemon & Garlic, while smooth, rich Chicken Liver Pâté is a specialty of French bistros. Tantalizingly aromatic Soy Chicken Wings are a typical Chinese snack, irresistibly messy to eat.

A chicken salad can be as simple as you like, but it need not be dull. Chicken and bleu cheese are natural partners, as you will discover if you try Chicken, Cheese & Arugula Salad or Chicken Pinwheels with Bleu Cheese & Herbs. Chicken loves spices, too—Cajun Chicken Salad and Red Chicken Salad are great examples of this. And if you want a chicken salad that is very low in fat but big on style, try the Thai Chicken Salad— it looks and tastes so good, you certainly won't feel deprived!

chicken & broccoli soup

ingredients

SERVES 4–6

8 oz/225 g head broccoli
salt and pepper
2 oz/55 g unsalted butter
1 onion, chopped
8 oz/225 g/1⅓ cups
    basmati rice
8 oz/225 g skinless, boneless
    chicken breast, cut into
    thin slivers
1 oz/25 g/scant ¼ cup all-
    purpose whole wheat flour
10 fl oz/300 ml/1¼ cups milk
16 fl oz/500 ml/2 cups
    chicken stock
2 oz/55 g/generous ⅓ cup
    corn kernels

method

1 Break the broccoli into small florets and cook in a pan of lightly salted boiling water for 3 minutes, drain, then plunge into cold water and set aside.

2 Melt the butter in a pan over medium heat, add the onion, rice, and chicken, and cook for 5 minutes, stirring frequently.

3 Remove the pan from the heat and stir in the flour. Return to the heat and cook for 2 minutes, stirring constantly. Stir in the milk and then the stock. Bring to a boil, stirring constantly, then reduce the heat and let simmer for 10 minutes.

4 Drain the broccoli and add to the pan with the corn, salt, and pepper. Let simmer for 5 minutes, or until the rice is tender, then serve.

chicken & tarragon soup

ingredients

SERVES 4

2 oz/55 g unsalted butter

1 large onion, chopped

10^1/$_2$ oz/300 g cooked
    skinless chicken,
    shredded finely

20 fl oz/625 ml/2^1/$_2$ cups
    chicken stock

salt and pepper

1 tbsp chopped fresh tarragon

5 fl oz/150 ml/^{2}/$_3$ cup
    heavy cream

fresh tarragon leaves, to garnish

deep-fried croutons, to serve

method

1 Melt the butter in a large pan and fry the onion for 3 minutes.

2 Add the chicken to the pan with half of the chicken stock. Bring to a boil, then reduce the heat and let simmer for 20 minutes. Let cool, then process until smooth in a blender or food processor.

3 Add the remainder of the stock and season with salt and pepper.

4 Add the chopped tarragon, then transfer the soup to individual serving bowls and stir in the cream.

5 Garnish the soup with fresh tarragon and serve with deep-fried croutons.

chicken, avocado & chipotle soup

ingredients

SERVES 4

50 fl oz/1.6 litres/6¼ cups
   chicken stock
2–3 garlic cloves, finely
   chopped
1–2 dried chipotle chiles, cut
   into very thin strips
1 avocado
lime or lemon juice, for tossing
3–5 scallions, thinly sliced
12–14 oz/350–400 g cooked
   chicken breast meat, torn or
   cut into shreds or thin strips
2 tbsp chopped fresh cilantro
1 lime, cut into wedges, and
   handful of tortilla chips
   (optional), to serve

method

1 Place the stock in a large, heavy-bottom pan with the garlic and chiles and bring to a boil.

2 Meanwhile, cut the avocado in half around the pit. Twist apart, then remove the pit with a knife. Carefully peel off the skin, dice the flesh, and immediately toss in lime juice to prevent discoloration.

3 Arrange the scallions, chicken, avocado, and cilantro in the bottom of 4 soup bowls or in a large serving bowl.

4 Ladle the hot stock over and serve with lime wedges and a handful of tortilla chips, if wished.

clear soup with mushrooms & chicken

ingredients

SERVES 4

1 oz/25 g/$^1/_4$ cup dried cèpes
   or other mushrooms

32 fl oz/1 liter/4 cups water

2 tbsp vegetable or peanut oil

4 oz mushrooms, sliced

2 garlic cloves, chopped
   coarsely

2-inch piece fresh galangal,
   sliced thinly

2 chicken breast portions
   (on the bone, skin on)

8 oz baby cremini or white
   mushrooms, cut into
   fourths

juice of $^1/_2$ lime

sprigs fresh flat-leaf parsley,
   to garnish

method

1 Place the dried mushrooms in a small bowl and pour over hot water to cover. Set aside to soak for 20–30 minutes. Drain the mushrooms, reserving the soaking liquid. Cut off and discard the stalks and chop the caps coarsely.

2 Pour the reserved soaking water into a pan with the measured water and bring to a boil. Reduce the heat to a simmer.

3 Meanwhile, heat the oil in a wok and stir-fry the soaked mushrooms, sliced fresh mushrooms, garlic, and galangal for 3–4 minutes. Add to the pan of hot water with the chicken breasts. Let simmer for 10–15 minutes, until the meat comes off the bones easily.

4 Remove the chicken from the pan. Peel off and set aside the skin. Remove the meat from the bones, slice, and set aside. Return the skin and bones to the stock and let simmer for an additional 30 minutes.

5 Remove the pan from the heat and strain the stock into a clean pan through a lined strainer lined with cheesecloth. Bring back to a boil and add the cremini or white mushrooms, sliced chicken, and lime juice. Reduce the heat and let simmer for 8-10 minutes. Ladle into warmed bowls, garnish with parsley sprigs, and serve immediately.

thai chicken-coconut soup

ingredients

SERVES 4

4 oz/115 g dried
   cellophane noodles

40 fl oz/1.25 liters/5 cups
   chicken or
   vegetable stock

1 lemongrass stalk, crushed

1/2-inch/1-cm piece fresh
   gingerroot, peeled and
   very finely chopped

2 fresh kaffir lime leaves,
   thinly sliced

1 fresh red chile, or to taste,
   seeded and thinly sliced

2 skinless, boneless chicken
   breasts, thinly sliced

8 oz/225 g/1 cup
   coconut cream

2 tbsp nam pla (Thai fish sauce)

about 1 tbsp fresh lime juice

2 oz/55 g/scant 1/2 cup
   bean sprouts

green part of 4 scallions,
   finely sliced

fresh cilantro leaves,
   to garnish

method

1 Soak the dried noodles in a large bowl with enough lukewarm water to cover for 20 minutes, until soft. Alternatively, cook according to the package instructions. Drain well and set aside.

2 Meanwhile, bring the stock to a boil in a large pan over high heat. Lower the heat, add the lemongrass, gingerroot, lime leaves, and chile and let simmer for 5 minutes. Add the chicken and continue simmering for an additional 3 minutes, or until the flesh is poached. Stir in the coconut cream, nam pla, and most of the lime juice and continue simmering for 3 minutes. Add the bean sprouts and scallions and let simmer for an additional 1 minute. Taste and gradually add extra nam pla or lime juice at this point, if you like. Remove and discard the lemongrass stalk.

3 Divide the noodles among 4 bowls. Bring the soup back to a boil, then add the soup to each bowl. The heat of the soup will warm the noodles. To garnish, sprinkle with cilantro leaves.

chicken-noodle soup

ingredients

SERVES 4–6

2 skinless chicken breasts

64 fl oz/2 liters/8 cups water

1 onion, with skin left on,
  cut in half

1 large garlic clove, cut in half

$^1/_2$-inch/1-cm piece fresh
  gingerroot, peeled
  and sliced

4 black peppercorns, lightly
  crushed

4 cloves

2 star anise

salt and pepper

1 carrot, peeled

1 celery stalk, chopped

$3^1/_2$ oz/100 g baby corn, cut
  in half lengthwise and
  chopped

2 scallions, finely shredded

4 oz/115 g dried rice
  vermicelli noodles

method

1 Put the chicken breasts and water in a pan over high heat and bring to a boil. Lower the heat to its lowest setting and let simmer, skimming the surface until no more foam rises. Add the onion, garlic, gingerroot, peppercorns, cloves, star anise, and a pinch of salt and continue to simmer for 20 minutes, or until the chicken is tender and cooked through. Meanwhile, grate the carrot along its length on the coarse side of a grater so you get long, thin strips.

2 Strain the chicken, reserving about 40 fl oz/ 1.25 liters/5 cups stock, but discarding any flavoring ingredients. (At this point you can let the stock cool and refrigerate overnight, so any fat solidifies and can be lifted off and discarded.) Return the stock to the rinsed-out pan with the carrot, celery, baby corn, and scallions and bring to a boil. Boil until the baby corn are almost tender, then add the noodles and continue boiling for 2 minutes.

3 Meanwhile, chop the chicken, add it to the pan, and continue cooking for about 1 minute until the chicken is reheated and the noodles are soft. Add seasoning.

whole chicken soup

ingredients

SERVES 6–8

3^1/2 oz/100 g Yunnan ham or
   ordinary ham, chopped

2 dried Chinese mushrooms,
   soaked in warm water for
   20 minutes

3 oz/85 g/^{3}/4 cup fresh or
   canned bamboo shoots,
   rinsed (if using fresh
   shoots, boil in water first
   for 30 minutes)

1 whole chicken

1 tbsp slivered scallion

8 slices fresh gingerroot

8 oz/225 g lean pork, chopped

2 tsp Shaoxing rice wine

96 fl oz/2.8 liters/12 cups
   water

2 tsp salt

10^1/2 oz/300 g Chinese
   cabbage, cut into
   large chunks

sesame & scallion dipping sauce

2 tbsp light soy sauce

^{1}/4 tsp sesame oil

2 tsp finely chopped scallion

method

1 To make the dipping sauce, combine all the ingredients in a small bowl and set aside.

2 Blanch the Yunnan ham in boiling water for 30 seconds. Skim the surface, then remove the ham and set aside. Squeeze out any excess water from the mushrooms, then finely slice, discarding any tough stems. Chop the bamboo shoots into small cubes.

3 Stuff the chicken with the scallion and gingerroot. Put all the ingredients, except the cabbage and dipping sauce, in a casserole. Bring to a boil, then lower the heat and let simmer, covered, for 1 hour. Add the cabbage and simmer for an additional 3 minutes.

4 Remove the chicken skin before serving, then place a chunk of chicken meat in each individual bowl, adding pieces of vegetable and the other meats, and pour the soup on top. Serve with the dipping sauce.

chicken crostini

ingredients

SERVES 4

12 slices French bread or
   country bread
4 tbsp olive oil
2 garlic cloves, chopped
2 tbsp finely chopped fresh
   oregano
salt and pepper
3$^{1}/_{2}$ oz/100 g cold roast
   chicken, cut into small,
   thin slices
4 tomatoes, sliced
12 thin slices of goat cheese
12 black olives, pitted
   and chopped
fresh red and green salad
   leaves, to serve

method

1 Put the bread under a preheated medium broiler and lightly toast on both sides. Meanwhile, pour the olive oil into a bowl and add the garlic and oregano. Season with salt and pepper and mix well. Remove the toasted bread slices from the broiler and brush them on one side only with the oil mixture.

2 Place the bread slices, oiled sides up, on a cookie sheet. Put some sliced chicken on top of each one, followed by a slice of tomato.

3 Divide the slices of goat cheese among the bread slices, then top with the chopped olives. Drizzle over the remaining oil mixture and transfer to a preheated oven, 350°F/ 180°C. Bake for about 5 minutes, or until the cheese is golden and starting to melt.

4 Remove from the oven and serve on a bed of fresh red and green salad leaves.

crispy chicken & ham croquettes

ingredients

MAKES 8

4 tbsp olive oil

4 tbsp all-purpose flour

7 fl oz/200 ml/scant
   1 cup milk

4 oz/115 g cooked chicken,
   ground

2 oz/55 g serrano or cooked
   ham, very finely chopped

1 tbsp chopped fresh
   flat-leaf parsley, plus extra
   sprigs to garnish

small pinch of freshly
   grated nutmeg

salt and pepper

1 egg, beaten

2 oz/55 g/1 cup day-old white
   bread crumbs

corn oil, for deep-frying

garlic mayonnaise, to serve

method

1 Heat the olive oil in a pan. Stir in the flour to form a paste and cook gently for 1 minute, stirring constantly. Gradually stir in the milk until smooth and slowly bring to a boil, stirring, until the mixture boils and thickens.

2 Remove from the heat, add the ground chicken, and beat until the mixture is smooth. Add the chopped ham, parsley, and nutmeg and mix well together. Season with salt and pepper. Put in a dish and let stand for 30 minutes, until cool, then cover and let rest in the refrigerator for 2–3 hours or overnight.

3 Pour the beaten egg onto a plate and spread out the bread crumbs on another plate. Divide the chilled chicken mixture into 8 portions, then shape to form cylindrical croquettes. Dip them, one at a time, in the beaten egg, then roll in the bread crumbs to coat. Let chill in the refrigerator for 1 hour.

4 Heat the oil in a deep-fryer to 350–375°F/ 180–190°C. Add the croquettes, in batches to prevent the temperature of the oil dropping, and deep-fry for 5–10 minutes, or until golden brown and crispy. Remove with a slotted spoon and drain well on paper towels.

5 Serve the croquettes piping hot, garnished with parsley sprigs, with garlic mayonnaise.

chicken liver pâté

ingredients

MAKES 8–10 SLICES

6 oz/175 g unsalted butter

1 lb 2 oz/500 g chicken livers,
thawed if frozen,
and trimmed

1/2 tbsp sunflower oil

2 shallots, finely chopped

2 large garlic cloves, finely
chopped

2 1/2 tbsp Madeira or brandy

2 tbsp heavy cream

1 tsp dried thyme

1/4 tsp ground allspice

salt and pepper

toasted slices brioche and
mixed salad greens, to
serve

method

1 Melt 1 oz/30 g of the butter in a large skillet over medium-high heat. Add the chicken livers and stir for 5 minutes, or until they are brown on the outside, but still slightly pink in the centers. Work in batches, if necessary, to avoid overcrowding the pan.

2 Transfer the livers and their cooking juices to a food processor. Melt another 1 oz/30 g of the butter with the oil in the pan. Add the shallots and garlic and sauté, stirring frequently, for 2–3 minutes, until the shallots are soft, but not brown.

3 Add the Madeira and scrape up any cooking juices from the base. Stir in the cream, then the thyme, allspice, salt, and pepper. Pour this mixture, with the cooking juices, into the food processor with the livers. Add the remaining butter, cut into small pieces.

4 Whiz the mixture in the food processor until smooth. Taste, and adjust the seasoning if necessary. Let the mixture cool slightly, then scrape into a serving bowl and set aside to allow the pâté to cool completely.

5 Serve immediately, or cover and store in the refrigerator for up to 3 days and let stand at room temperature for 30 minutes before serving. Serve with hot toasted brioche and mixed salad greens.

chicken in lemon & garlic

ingredients

SERVES 6–8

4 large skinless, boneless
  chicken breasts
5 tbsp Spanish olive oil
1 onion, finely chopped
6 garlic cloves,
  finely chopped
grated rind of 1 lemon, finely
  pared zest of 1 lemon and
  juice of both lemons
4 tbsp chopped fresh
  flat-leaf parsley, plus extra
  to garnish
salt and pepper
lemon wedges and crusty
  bread, to serve

method

1 Using a sharp knife, slice the chicken breasts widthwise into very thin slices. Heat the olive oil in a large, heavy-bottom skillet, add the onion and cook for 5 minutes, or until softened, but not browned. Add the garlic and cook for an additional 30 seconds.

2 Add the sliced chicken to the skillet and cook gently for 5–10 minutes, stirring from time to time, until all the ingredients are lightly browned and the chicken is tender.

3 Add the grated lemon rind and the lemon juice and let it bubble. At the same time, deglaze the skillet by scraping and stirring all the bits on the bottom of the skillet into the juices with a wooden spoon. Remove the skillet from the heat, stir in the parsley, and season with salt and pepper.

4 Transfer, piping hot, to a warmed serving dish. Sprinkle with the pared lemon zest, garnish with the parsley, and serve with lemon wedges for squeezing over the chicken, accompanied by chunks or slices of crusty bread for mopping up the juices.

soy chicken wings

ingredients

SERVES 3–4

9 oz/250 g chicken wings, defrosted if frozen

8 fl oz/250 ml/1 cup water

1 tbsp sliced scallion

1-inch/2.5-cm piece of fresh gingerroot, cut into 4 slices

2 tbsp light soy sauce

$1/2$ tsp dark soy sauce

1 star anise

1 tsp sugar

method

1 Wash and dry the chicken wings. In a small pan, bring the water to a boil, then add the chicken, scallion, and gingerroot and bring back to a boil.

2 Add the remaining ingredients, then cover and simmer for 30 minutes.

3 Using a slotted spoon, remove the chicken wings from any remaining liquid and serve hot.

mixed greens with warm chicken livers

ingredients

SERVES 4 AS AN ENTRÉE

9 oz/250 g mixed salad
   greens, torn into bite-size
   pieces
2 tbsp chopped fresh
   flat-leaf parsley
2 tbsp snipped fresh chives
3–4 tbsp olive oil
3^1/$_2$ oz/100 g shallots,
   finely chopped
1 large garlic clove,
   finely chopped
1 lb 2 oz/500 g chicken
   livers, cored, trimmed
   and halved
3 tbsp raspberry vinegar
salt and pepper
French bread, to serve

method

1 Toss the salad greens with the parsley and chives and divide among individual plates.

2 Heat 2 tablespoons of the oil in a sauté pan or skillet over medium–high heat. Add the shallots and garlic and sauté for 2 minutes, or until the shallots are soft, but not brown.

3 Add an extra tablespoon of the oil to the sauté pan and heat. Add the chicken livers and sauté for 5 minutes, or until they appear just pink in the center when cut in half. Add a little extra oil to the pan while the chicken livers are sautéeing, if necessary.

4 Increase the heat to high, then add the raspberry vinegar and stir quickly. Season with salt and pepper, then spoon the livers and cooking juices over the mixed greens. Serve immediately with French bread.

cheese
a salad

2 celery,
and sliced

1/2 cucumber, sliced

2 scallions, trimmed
and sliced

2 tbsp chopped
fresh parsley

1 oz/25 g walnut pieces

12 oz/350 g boneless roast
chicken, sliced

4 1/2 oz/125 g Stilton cheese,
cubed

handful of seedless
red grapes, cut in
half (optional)

salt and pepper

dressing

2 tbsp olive oil

1 tbsp sherry vinegar

1 tsp Dijon mustard

1 tbsp chopped
mixed herbs

method

1 Wash the arugula leaves, pat dry with paper towels, and put them into a large salad bowl. Add the celery, cucumber, scallions, parsley, and walnuts and mix together well. Transfer onto a large serving platter. Arrange the chicken slices over the salad, then scatter over the cheese. Add the red grapes, if using. Season well with salt and pepper.

2 To make the dressing, put all the ingredients into a screw-top jar and shake well. Alternatively, put them into a bowl and mix together well. Drizzle the dressing over the salad and serve.

roast chicken salad with orange dressing

ingredients

SERVES 4

9 oz/250 g young spinach
    leaves
handful of fresh parsley leaves
$^1/_2$ cucumber, thinly sliced
$3^1/_4$ oz/90 g/generous $^3/_4$ cup
    walnuts, toasted and
    chopped
12 oz/350 g boneless lean
    roast chicken, thinly sliced
2 red apples
1 tbsp lemon juice
fresh flat-leaf parsley sprigs,
    to garnish
orange wedges, to serve

orange dressing

2 tbsp extra-virgin olive oil
juice of 1 orange
finely grated rind
    of $^1/_2$ orange
1 tbsp sour cream

method

1 Wash and drain the spinach and parsley leaves, if necessary, then arrange on a large serving platter. Top with the cucumber and walnuts. Arrange the chicken slices on top of the leaves.

2 Core the apples, then cut them in half. Cut each half into slices and brush with the lemon juice to prevent discoloration. Arrange the apple slices over the salad.

3 Place all the dressing ingredients in a screw-top jar, screw on the lid tightly, and shake well until thoroughly combined. Drizzle the dressing over the salad, garnish with parsley sprigs, and serve immediately with orange wedges.

chicken pinwheels with bleu cheese & herbs

ingredients

SERVES 4

2 tbsp pine nuts, lightly toasted

2 tbsp chopped fresh parsley

2 tbsp chopped fresh thyme

1 garlic clove, chopped

1 tbsp grated lemon rind

salt and pepper

4 large, skinless chicken breasts

9 oz/250 g bleu cheese, such as Stilton, crumbled

twists of lemon and sprigs of fresh thyme, to garnish

fresh green and red salad leaves, to serve

method

1 Put the pine nuts into a food processor with the parsley, thyme, garlic, and lemon rind. Season with salt and pepper.

2 Pound the chicken breasts lightly to flatten them. Spread them on one side with the pine nut mixture, then top with the cheese. Roll them up from one short end to the other, so that the filling is enclosed. Wrap the rolls individually in aluminum foil, and seal well. Transfer to a steamer, or a metal colander placed over a pan of boiling water, cover tightly, and steam for 10–12 minutes, or until cooked through.

3 Arrange the salad leaves on a large serving platter. Remove the chicken from the heat, discard the foil, and cut the chicken rolls into slices. Arrange the slices over the salad leaves, garnish with twists of lemon and sprigs of thyme, and serve.

cajun chicken salad

ingredients

SERVES 4

4 skinless, boneless chicken
   breasts, about 5 oz/
   140 g each
4 tsp Cajun seasoning
2 tsp corn oil (optional)
1 ripe mango, peeled, pitted,
   and cut into thick slices
7 oz/200 g mixed salad greens
1 red onion, thinly sliced and
   cut in half
6 oz/175 g cooked beet, diced
3 oz/85 g radishes, sliced
2 oz/55 g/scant $1/2$ cup walnut
   halves
4 tbsp walnut oil
1–2 tsp Dijon mustard
1 tbsp lemon juice
salt and pepper
2 tbsp sesame seeds

method

1 Make 3 diagonal slashes across each chicken breast. Put the chicken into a shallow dish and sprinkle all over with the Cajun seasoning. Cover and let chill for at least 30 minutes.

2 When ready to cook, brush a grill pan with the corn oil, if using. Heat over high heat until very hot and a few drops of water sprinkled into the pan sizzle immediately. Add the chicken and cook for 7–8 minutes on each side, or until thoroughly cooked. If still slightly pink in the center, cook a little longer. Remove the chicken and set aside.

3 Add the mango slices to the pan and cook for 2 minutes on each side. Remove from the pan and set aside.

4 Meanwhile, arrange the salad greens in a salad bowl, reserving a few for a garnish, and sprinkle over the onion, beet, radishes, and walnut halves.

5 Put the walnut oil, mustard, lemon juice, salt, and pepper in a screw-top jar and shake until well blended. Pour over the salad and sprinkle with the sesame seeds.

6 Arrange the mango and the salad on a serving plate, top with the chicken breast and garnish with a few of the salad greens.

chicken with water chestnuts & plum sauce

ingredients

SERVES 4–6

1 tbsp vegetable or
   groundnut oil

3¹/₂ oz/100 g chicken, finely
   chopped

1 oz/25 g water chestnuts,
   finely chopped

1 tsp finely chopped Chinese
   chives

1 oz/25 g pine nuts, lightly
   toasted

1 tsp salt

¹/₂ tsp white pepper

6 salad leaves, washed

3 tsp plum sauce, to serve

method

1 In a preheated wok or deep pan, heat the oil and stir-fry the chicken for 1 minute. Add the water chestnuts and chives and cook for 2 minutes. Add the pine nuts and cook for 1 minute. Add the salt and pepper and stir.

2 To serve, place a spoonful in the center of each salad leaf, top with the plum sauce, and fold the lettuce leaf to make a small roll.

gingered chicken & vegetable salad

ingredients

SERVES 4

4 skinless, boneless chicken
   breasts
4 scallions, chopped
1-inch/2.5-cm piece
   gingerroot, chopped finely
2 garlic cloves, crushed
2 tbsp vegetable or peanut oil

salad

1 tbsp vegetable or peanut oil
1 onion, sliced
2 garlic cloves, chopped
4 oz/115 g baby corn, halved
4 oz/115 g snow peas, halved
   lengthwise
1 red bell pepper, seeded
   and sliced
3-inch/7.5-cm piece
   cucumber, peeled,
   seeded, and sliced
4 tbsp Thai soy sauce
1 tbsp jaggery or soft light
   brown sugar
few Thai basil leaves
6 oz fine egg noodles

method

1 Cut the chicken into large cubes, each about 1 inch. Mix the scallions, gingerroot, garlic, and oil together in a shallow dish and add the chicken. Cover and let marinate for at least 3 hours. Lift the meat out of the marinade and set aside.

2 To make the salad, heat the oil in a wok or large skillet and cook the onion for 1–2 minutes before adding the rest of the vegetables, except the cucumber. Cook for 2–3 minutes, until just tender. Add the cucumber, half the soy sauce, the sugar, and the basil, and mix gently.

3 Meanwhile, soak the noodles for 2–3 minutes (check the package instructions) or until tender, and drain well. Sprinkle the remaining soy sauce over them and arrange on plates. Top with the cooked vegetables.

4 Add a little more oil to the wok, if necessary, and cook the chicken over fairly high heat until browned on all sides. Arrange the chicken cubes on top of the salad and serve hot or warm.

chicken-sesame salad

ingredients

SERVES 4

7 oz/200 g dried thick
Chinese egg noodles

$3^1/_2$ oz/100 g snow peas

2 celery stalks

4 cooked skinless chicken
thighs

sesame dressing

3 tbsp dark soy sauce

3 tbsp Chinese sesame paste

$^1/_2$ tbsp bottled hoisin sauce

$^1/_2$ tbsp sugar

$^1/_2$–1 tbsp bottled sweet chili
sauce, to taste

1 tsp rice wine

$^1/_2$ tbsp boiling water

method

1 To make the dressing, whisk the soy sauce, sesame paste, hoisin sauce, sugar, chili sauce, and rice wine together, then whisk in the boiling water and continue whisking until the sugar dissolves. Let the dressing stand until it is cool, then cover and let chill until required.

2 Meanwhile, cook the noodles in boiling water for 5 minutes (check the package instructions), until soft. Drain, rinse with cold water to stop the cooking, and drain again. Set aside.

3 Use a small, sharp knife to slice the snow peas lengthwise into thin strips, and cut the celery into thin strips. Use your hands to pull the chicken into thin shreds. If you aren't serving the salad straightaway, cover the chicken and vegetables and let chill.

4 When you are ready to serve, put the noodles, chicken, snow peas, and celery in a large bowl. Toss together so all the ingredients are mixed and pour the dressing on top.

red chicken salad

ingredients

SERVES 4

4 boneless chicken breasts

2 tbsp red curry paste

2 tbsp vegetable or peanut oil

1 head Napa cabbage,
   shredded

6 oz/175 g bok choy, torn into
   large pieces

1/2 savoy cabbage, shredded

2 shallots, chopped finely

2 garlic cloves, crushed

1 tbsp rice wine vinegar

2 tbsp sweet chili sauce

2 tbsp Thai soy sauce

method

1 Slash the flesh of the chicken several times and rub the curry paste into each cut. Cover and let chill overnight.

2 Cook in a heavy-bottom pan over medium heat or on a grill pan for 5–6 minutes, turning once or twice, until cooked through. Keep warm.

3 Heat 1 tablespoon of the oil in a wok or large skillet and stir-fry the Napa cabbage, bok choy, and savoy cabbage until just wilted. Add the remaining oil, shallots, and garlic, and stir-fry until just tender, but not browned. Add the vinegar, chili sauce, and soy. Remove from the heat.

4 Arrange the leaves on 4 serving plates. Slice the chicken, arrange on the salad greens, and drizzle the hot dressing over. Serve immediately.

thai chicken salad

ingredients

SERVES 6

vegetable oil spray

4 oz/115g skinless chicken
   breast, cut lengthwise
   horizontally

3 limes

dressing

1 tbsp finely shredded
   lemongrass

1 small green chile, finely
   chopped

3 tbsp lime juice

$1/2$-inch/1-cm galangal or
   gingerroot, peeled and
   thinly sliced into strips

$1^1/_2$ tsp sugar

2 tbsp white wine vinegar

3 fl oz water

$1^1/_2$ tsp cornstarch

salad

1 oz/25 g rice vermicelli

$1^3/_4$ oz/50 g mixed bell
   peppers, seeded

$1^3/_4$ oz/50 g carrot

$1^3/_4$ oz/50 g zucchini

$1^3/_4$ oz/50 g snow peas

$1^3/_4$ oz/50 g baby corn

$1^3/_4$ oz/50 g broccoli florets

$1^3/_4$ oz/50 g bok choy

4 tbsp roughly chopped fresh
   cilantro leaves

method

1 To make the dressing, put all the dressing ingredients, except the cornstarch, into a small pan over low heat and bring to a boil. Blend the cornstarch with a little cold water, gradually add to the pan, stirring constantly, and cook until thickened. Remove from the heat and let cool.

2 Heat a grill pan over high heat and spray lightly with oil. Add the chicken and cook for 2 minutes on each side, or until thoroughly cooked through. Remove the chicken from the pan and shred.

3 To make the salad, cover the rice vermicelli with boiling water then let it cool in the water. Meanwhile, finely slice the bell peppers, carrot, zucchini, snow peas, and baby corn into strips. Cut the broccoli florets into $1/4$-inch/5-mm pieces and shred the bok choy. Drain the rice vermicelli and put all the salad ingredients with the chicken into a large bowl. Pour over the dressing and toss together, making sure that all the ingredients are well coated.

4 Cover and refrigerate for at least 2 hours before serving. Serve with the juice from half a lime squeezed over each portion.

lunch
& light meals

Chicken is quick to cook and very easily digested, making it the perfect meat to use for a light lunch or evening meal. One of the fastest and most nutritious options is a stir-fry, which can be prepared and cooked in minutes and served with rice, noodles, or a satisfying bread such as naan. Stir-fries are also good because everything goes into the wok, including the vegetables and flavorings, so you only have one pan to deal with—great for all those occasions when you're in a hurry but still want something 'proper' to eat! Try Five-spice Chicken with Vegetables, Sweet-&-Sour Chicken, or Chicken with Bok Choy, which is ideal for a low-carb diet.

Curries are also quick to make, and look as if you've put in hours of effort. The Creamy Chicken Curry with Lemon Rice, or Balti Chicken, are impressive dishes to serve when you have friends coming for a midweek dinner; or give them Chicken Breasts with Coconut Milk, Gingered Chicken Kabobs, or Bacon-wrapped Chicken Burgers, all of which can be prepared in advance.

For something a little more exciting than a sandwich, choose Chicken Fajitas or Chicken Tacos from Puebla. If a lowfat recipe is what you're after, Chicken Wraps, Lime Chicken with Mint, and Pan-fried Chicken & Cilantro are all designed with you in mind!

shredded chicken & mixed mushrooms

ingredients

SERVES 4

2 tbsp vegetable or peanut oil

2 skinless, boneless chicken
   breasts

1 red onion, sliced

2 garlic cloves, chopped finely

1-inch/2.5-cm piece fresh
   gingerroot, grated

4 oz/115 g baby white
   mushrooms

4 oz/115 g shiitake
   mushrooms, halved

4 oz/115 g cremini
   mushrooms, sliced

2–3 tbsp green curry paste

2 tbsp Thai soy sauce

4 tbsp chopped fresh parsley

boiled noodles or rice, to serve

method

1 Heat the oil in a wok and cook the chicken on all sides until lightly browned and cooked through. Remove with a slotted spoon, shred into even-size pieces, and set aside.

2 Pour off any excess oil, then stir-fry the onion, garlic, and gingerroot for 1–2 minutes, or until softened. Add all the mushrooms and stir-fry for 2–3 minutes, until they start to brown.

3 Add the curry paste, soy sauce, and shredded chicken to the wok and stir-fry for 1–2 minutes. Stir in the parsley and serve immediately with boiled noodles or rice.

five-spice chicken with vegetables

ingredients

SERVES 4

2 tbsp sesame oil

1 garlic clove, chopped

3 scallions, trimmed
    and sliced

1 tbsp cornstarch

2 tbsp rice wine

4 skinless chicken breasts,
    cut into strips

1 tbsp Chinese
    five-spice powder

1 tbsp grated fresh gingerroot

4 fl oz/125 ml/^{1}/$_2$ cup
    chicken stock

3^1/$_2$ oz/100 g baby corn cobs,
    sliced

10^1/$_2$ oz/300 g/3 cups
    bean sprouts

finely chopped scallions,
    to garnish, optional

freshly cooked jasmine rice,
    to serve

method

1 Heat the oil in a preheated wok or large skillet. Add the garlic and scallions and stir-fry over medium-high heat for 1 minute.

2 In a bowl, mix together the cornstarch and rice wine, then add the mixture to the pan. Stir-fry for 1 minute, then add the chicken, five-spice powder, gingerroot, and chicken stock and cook for another 4 minutes. Add the corn cobs and cook for 2 minutes, then add the bean sprouts and cook for another minute.

3 Remove from the heat, garnish with chopped scallions, if using, and serve with freshly cooked jasmine rice.

chicken & ginger stir-fry

ingredients

SERVES 4

3 tbsp vegetable oil

1 lb 9 oz/700 g lean skinless,
  boneless chicken breasts,
  cut into 2-inch/5-cm strips

3 garlic cloves, crushed

1 tsp pomegranate
  seeds, crushed

1$^1/_2$-inch/3.5-cm piece
  fresh gingerroot, cut
  into strips

$^1/_2$ tsp turmeric

1 tsp garam masala

2 fresh green chiles, sliced

$^1/_2$ tsp salt

4 tbsp lemon juice

grated rind of 1 lemon

6 tbsp chopped fresh cilantro,
  plus extra to garnish

4 fl oz/125 ml/$^1/_2$ cup
  chicken stock

naan bread, to serve

method

1 Heat the oil in a preheated wok or large skillet. Add the chicken and stir-fry until golden brown all over. Remove from the wok and set aside.

2 Add the garlic, pomegranate seeds, and gingerroot to the wok and stir-fry in the oil for 1 minute, taking care not to let the garlic burn.

3 Stir in the turmeric, garam masala, and chiles and fry for 30 seconds.

4 Return the chicken to the wok and add the salt, lemon juice, lemon rind, cilantro, and stock. Stir the chicken well to make sure it is coated in the sauce.

5 Bring the mixture to a boil, then reduce the heat and let simmer for 10–15 minutes, or until the chicken is thoroughly cooked. Garnish with chopped cilantro and serve with warm naan bread.

chicken with bok choy

ingredients

SERVES 4

6 oz/175 g broccoli

1 tbsp peanut oil

1-inch/2.5-cm piece fresh
   gingerroot, finely grated

1 fresh red Thai chile, seeded
   and chopped

2 garlic cloves, crushed

1 red onion, cut into wedges

1 lb/450 g skinless, boneless
   chicken breast, cut into
   thin strips

6 oz/175 g bok choy,
   shredded

4 oz/115 g baby corn, halved

1 tbsp light soy sauce

1 tbsp Thai fish sauce

1 tbsp chopped fresh cilantro

1 tbsp toasted sesame seeds

method

1 Break the broccoli into small florets and cook in a pan of lightly salted boiling water for 3 minutes. Drain and set aside.

2 Heat a wok over high heat until almost smoking, add the oil, and then add the gingerroot, chile, and garlic. Stir-fry for 1 minute. Add the onion and chicken and stir-fry for an additional 3–4 minutes, or until the chicken is sealed on all sides.

3 Add the remaining vegetables to the wok, including the broccoli, and stir-fry for 3–4 minutes, or until tender.

4 Add the soy and Thai fish sauces to the wok and stir-fry for an additional 1–2 minutes, then serve at once sprinkled with the cilantro and sesame seeds.

chicken satay

ingredients

SERVES 4

2 tbsp vegetable or peanut oil

1 tbsp sesame oil

juice of $^1/_2$ lime

2 skinless, boneless chicken
   breasts, cut into small cubes

dip

2 tbsp vegetable or peanut oil

1 small onion, chopped finely

1 small fresh green chile,
   seeded and chopped

1 garlic clove, chopped finely

4 oz/115 g/$^1/_2$ cup crunchy
   peanut butter

6–8 tbsp water

juice of $^1/_2$ lime

method

1 Combine both the oils and the lime juice in a nonmetallic dish. Add the chicken cubes, cover with plastic wrap, and let chill for 1 hour. Soak 8–12 wooden skewers in cold water for 30 minutes before use, to prevent burning.

2 To make the dip, heat the oil in a skillet and sauté the onion, chile, and garlic over low heat, stirring occasionally, for about 5 minutes, until just softened. Add the peanut butter, water, and lime juice and let simmer gently, stirring constantly, until the peanut butter has softened enough to make a dip— you may need to add extra water to make a thinner consistency.

3 Meanwhile, drain the chicken cubes and thread them onto the wooden skewers. Put under a hot broiler or on a barbecue, turning frequently, for about 10 minutes, until cooked and browned. Serve hot with the warm dip.

sweet-&-sour chicken

ingredients

SERVES 4–6

1 lb/450 g lean chicken meat, cubed

5 tbsp vegetable or peanut oil

$1/2$ tsp minced garlic

$1/2$ tsp finely chopped fresh gingerroot

1 green bell pepper, coarsely chopped

1 onion, coarsely chopped

1 carrot, finely sliced

1 tsp sesame oil

1 tbsp finely chopped scallion

freshly cooked rice, to serve

marinade

2 tsp light soy sauce

1 tsp Shaoxing rice wine

pinch of white pepper

$1/2$ tsp salt

dash of sesame oil

sauce

8 tbsp rice vinegar

4 tbsp sugar

2 tsp light soy sauce

6 tbsp tomato ketchup

method

1 Place all the marinade ingredients in a bowl and marinate the chicken pieces for at least 20 minutes.

2 To prepare the sauce, heat the vinegar in a pan and add the sugar, light soy sauce, and tomato ketchup. Stir to dissolve the sugar, then set aside.

3 In a preheated wok or deep pan, heat 3 tablespoons of the oil and stir-fry the chicken until it starts to turn golden brown. Remove and set aside.

4 In the clean wok or deep pan, heat the remaining oil and cook the garlic and gingerroot until fragrant. Add the vegetables and cook for 2 minutes. Add the chicken and cook for 1 minute. Finally add the sauce and sesame oil, then stir in the scallion and serve with rice.

chicken with yellow curry sauce

ingredients

SERVES 4

spice paste

6 tbsp yellow curry paste

5 fl oz/150 ml/^{2}/$_3$ cup plain
 yogurt

14 fl oz/425 ml/1^3/$_4$ cups
 water

handful of fresh cilantro,
 chopped, plus extra to
 garnish

handful of fresh Thai basil
 leaves, shredded, plus
 extra to garnish

stir-fry

2 tbsp vegetable or peanut oil

2 onions, cut into thin wedges

2 garlic cloves, chopped finely

2 skinless, boneless chicken
 breasts, cut into strips

6 oz baby corn, halved
 lengthwise

method

1 To make the spice paste, stir-fry the yellow curry paste in a wok for 2–3 minutes, then stir in the yogurt, water, and herbs. Bring to a boil, then let simmer for 2–3 minutes.

2 Meanwhile, heat the oil in a wok and stir-fry the onions and garlic for 2–3 minutes. Add the chicken and baby corn and stir-fry for 3–4 minutes, until the meat and baby corn are tender.

3 Stir in the spice paste and bring to a boil. Let simmer for 2–3 minutes, until heated through. Serve immediately, garnished with the extra herbs.

creamy chicken curry with lemon rice

ingredients

SERVES 4

2 tbsp vegetable oil

4 skinless, boneless chicken
   breasts, 1 lb 12 oz/800 g
   in total, cut into 1-inch/
   2.5-cm pieces

1$\frac{1}{2}$ tsp cumin seeds

1 large onion, grated

2 fresh green chiles, finely
   chopped

2 large garlic cloves, grated

1 tbsp grated fresh gingerroot

1 tsp ground turmeric

1 tsp ground coriander

1 tsp garam masala

10 fl oz/300 ml/1$\frac{1}{4}$ cups
   coconut milk

9 fl oz/250 ml canned
   chopped tomatoes

2 tsp lemon juice

salt

2 tbsp chopped fresh cilantro,
   to garnish

lemon rice

12 oz/350 g/scant 1$\frac{3}{4}$ cups
   basmati rice, rinsed

40 fl oz/1.25 liters/5 cups water

juice and grated rind of
   1 lemon

3 cloves

method

1 Heat the oil in a large, heavy-bottom pan over medium heat. Add the chicken and cook for 5–8 minutes, turning frequently, until lightly browned and cooked through. Remove from the pan and set aside. Add the cumin seeds and cook until they start to darken and sizzle. Stir in the onion, partially cover, and cook over medium-low heat, stirring frequently, for 10 minutes, or until soft and golden. Add the chiles, garlic, gingerroot, turmeric, ground coriander, and garam masala and cook for 1 minute.

2 Return the chicken to the pan and stir in the coconut milk and tomatoes. Partially cover and cook over medium heat for 15 minutes until the sauce has reduced and thickened. Stir in the lemon juice and season with salt.

3 Meanwhile, cook the rice. Put the rice into a pan and cover with the water. Add the lemon juice and cloves. Bring to a boil, then reduce the heat, cover, and let simmer over very low heat for 15 minutes, or until the rice is tender and all the water has been absorbed. Remove the pan from the heat and stir in the lemon rind. Let the rice stand, covered, for 5 minutes.

4 Serve the curry with the lemon rice, sprinkled with fresh cilantro.

chicken breasts with coconut milk

ingredients

SERVES 4

1 small onion, chopped
1 fresh green chile, seeded
    and chopped
1-inch/2.5-cm piece fresh
    gingerroot, chopped
2 tsp ground coriander
1 tsp ground cumin
1 tsp fennel seeds
1 tsp ground star anise
1 tsp cardamom seeds
$1/2$ tsp ground turmeric
$1/2$ tsp black peppercorns
$1/2$ tsp ground cloves
20 fl oz/625 ml/$2^1/2$ cups
    canned coconut milk
4 skinless, boneless chicken
    breast portions
vegetable oil, for brushing
fresh cilantro sprigs, to
    garnish
tomato rice and naan bread,
    to serve

method

1 Place the onion, chile, gingerroot, coriander, cumin, fennel seeds, star anise, cardamom seeds, turmeric, peppercorns, cloves, and 16 fl oz/500 ml/2 cups of the coconut milk in a food processor and process to make a paste, adding more coconut milk if necessary.

2 Using a sharp knife, slash the chicken breasts several times and place in a large, shallow, nonmetallic dish in a single layer. Pour over half the coconut milk mixture and turn to coat completely. Cover with plastic wrap and let marinate in the refrigerator for at least 1 hour, and up to 8 hours.

3 Heat a ridged grill pan and brush lightly with vegetable oil. Add the chicken, in batches if necessary, and cook for 6–7 minutes on each side, or until tender.

4 Meanwhile, pour the remaining coconut milk mixture into a pan and bring to a boil, stirring occasionally. Arrange the chicken in a warmed serving dish, spoon over a little of the coconut sauce, and garnish with cilantro sprigs. Serve hot with tomato rice and naan bread.

balti chicken

ingredients

SERVES 6

3 tbsp ghee or vegetable oil

2 large onions, sliced

3 tomatoes, sliced

1/2 tsp kalonji seeds

4 black peppercorns

2 cardamom pods

1 cinnamon stick

1 tsp chili powder

1 tsp garam masala

1 tsp garlic paste

1 tsp ginger paste

salt

1 lb 9 oz/700 g skinless,
   boneless chicken breasts
   or thighs, diced

2 tbsp plain yogurt

2 tbsp chopped fresh cilantro,
   plus extra to garnish

2 fresh green chiles, seeded
   and finely chopped

2 tbsp lime juice

naan bread, to serve

method

1 Heat the ghee in a large, heavy-bottom skillet. Add the onions and cook over low heat, stirring occasionally, for 10 minutes, or until golden. Add the sliced tomatoes, kalonji seeds, peppercorns, cardamoms, cinnamon stick, chili powder, garam masala, garlic paste, and ginger paste and season with salt. Cook, stirring constantly, for 5 minutes.

2 Add the chicken and cook, stirring constantly, for 5 minutes, or until well coated in the spice paste. Stir in the yogurt. Cover and let simmer, stirring occasionally, for 10 minutes.

3 Stir in the chopped cilantro, chiles, and lime juice. Transfer to a warmed serving dish, sprinkle with more chopped cilantro, and serve immediately with naan bread.

chicken with sesame sauce

ingredients

SERVES 4

12 oz/350 g boneless,
  skinless chicken meat
few drops of sesame oil
2 tbsp sesame paste
1 tbsp light soy sauce
1 tbsp chicken stock
$1/2$ tsp salt
pinch of sugar
8 tbsp shredded lettuce leaves
1 tbsp sesame seeds,
  roasted, to serve

method

1 Place the chicken in a pan of cold water, then bring to a boil and let simmer for 8–10 minutes. Drain and let cool a little, then cut or tear the chicken into bite-size pieces.

2 Mix together the sesame oil, sesame paste, light soy sauce, chicken stock, salt, and sugar and whisk until the sauce is thick and smooth. Toss in the chicken.

3 To serve, put the shredded lettuce on a large plate and spoon the chicken and sauce on top. Sprinkle with the sesame seeds and serve at room temperature.

lime chicken with mint

ingredients

SERVES 6

3 tbsp finely chopped
   fresh mint
4 tbsp honey
4 tbsp lime juice
salt and pepper
12 boneless chicken thighs
mixed salad, to serve

sauce

5 fl oz/150 ml/^{2}/$_3$ cup
   lowfat thick plain yogurt
1 tbsp finely chopped
   fresh mint
2 tsp finely grated lime rind

method

1 Mix the mint, honey, and lime juice in a large bowl and season with salt and pepper. Use toothpicks to keep the chicken thighs in neat shapes and add the chicken to the marinade, turning to coat evenly.

2 Cover with plastic wrap and let the chicken marinate in the refrigerator for at least 30 minutes. Remove the chicken from the marinade and drain. Set aside the marinade.

3 Preheat the broiler to medium. Place the chicken on a broiler rack and cook under the hot broiler for 15–18 minutes, or until the chicken is tender and the juices run clear when the tip of a knife is inserted into the thickest part of the meat, turning the chicken frequently and basting with the marinade.

4 Meanwhile, combine all the sauce ingredients in a bowl. Remove the toothpicks and serve with a mixed salad and the sauce, for dipping.

bacon-wrapped chicken burgers

ingredients

SERVES 4

1 lb/450 g fresh ground chicken

1 onion, grated

2 garlic cloves, crushed

2 oz/55 g/^{3}/$_8$ cup pine nuts, toasted

2 oz/55 g Gruyère cheese, grated

2 tbsp fresh snipped chives

salt and pepper

2 tbsp whole wheat flour

8 lean Canadian bacon slices

1–2 tbsp corn oil

method

1 Place the ground chicken, onion, garlic, pine nuts, cheese, chives, and salt and pepper in a food processor. Using the pulse button, blend the mixture together using short sharp bursts. Scrape out onto a board and shape into 4 even-size burgers. Coat in the flour, then cover and let chill for 1 hour.

2 Wrap each burger with 2 bacon slices, securing in place with a wooden toothpick.

3 Heat a heavy-bottom skillet and add the oil. When hot, add the burgers and cook over medium heat for 5–6 minutes on each side, or until thoroughly cooked through. Serve the burgers at once.

chicken fajitas

ingredients

SERVES 4

3 tbsp olive oil, plus extra
    for drizzling

3 tbsp maple syrup or honey

1 tbsp red wine vinegar

2 garlic cloves, crushed

2 tsp dried oregano

1–2 tsp dried
    red pepper flakes

salt and pepper

4 skinless, boneless
    chicken breasts

2 red bell peppers, seeded
    and cut into 1-inch/
    2.5-cm strips

8 flour tortillas, warmed

method

1 Place the oil, maple syrup, vinegar, garlic, oregano, pepper flakes, salt, and pepper in a large, shallow plate or bowl and mix together.

2 Slice the chicken across the grain into slices 1 inch/2.5 cm thick. Toss in the marinade until well coated. Cover and let chill in the refrigerator for 2–3 hours, turning occasionally.

3 Heat a grill pan until hot. Lift the chicken slices from the marinade with a slotted spoon, lay on the grill pan, and cook over medium-high heat for 3–4 minutes on each side, or until cooked through. Remove the chicken to a warmed serving plate and keep warm.

4 Add the bell peppers, skin-side down, to the grill pan, and cook for 2 minutes on each side. Transfer to the serving plate.

5 Serve at once with the warmed tortillas to be used as wraps.

chicken tacos from puebla

ingredients

SERVES 4

8 soft corn tortillas

2 tsp vegetable oil

8–12 oz/225–350 g leftover
  cooked chicken, diced
  or shredded

salt and pepper

8 oz/225 g canned refried
  beans, warmed with
  2 tbsp water to thin

$1/4$ tsp ground cumin

$1/4$ tsp dried oregano

1 avocado, pitted, peeled,
  sliced, and tossed with
  lime juice

salsa of your choice

1 canned chipotle chile in
  adobo marinade,
  chopped, or bottled
  chipotle salsa

6 fl oz/175 ml/$3/4$ cup
  sour cream

$1/2$ onion, chopped

handful of lettuce leaves

5 radishes, diced

method

1 Heat the tortillas through, in an unoiled nonstick skillet, in a stack, alternating the tortillas from the top to the bottom so that they warm evenly. Wrap in foil or a clean dish towel to keep them warm.

2 Heat the oil in a skillet. Add the chicken and heat through. Season with salt and pepper.

3 Combine the warmed refried beans with the cumin and oregano.

4 Spread one tortilla with the refried beans, then top with a spoonful of the chicken, a slice or two of avocado, a little salsa, chipotle to taste, a spoonful of sour cream, and a sprinkling of onion, lettuce, and radishes. Season with salt and pepper, then roll up as tightly as you can. Repeat with the remaining tortillas and serve at once.

chicken tostadas with green salsa & chipotle

ingredients

SERVES 4–6

6 soft corn tortillas

vegetable oil, for frying

1 lb/450 g skinned, boned
chicken breast or thigh,
cut into strips or small
pieces

8 fl oz/250 ml/1 cup
chicken stock

2 garlic cloves, finely chopped

14 oz/400 g canned
refried beans

large pinch of ground cumin

8 oz/225 g/2 cups grated
cheese

1 tbsp chopped fresh cilantro

2 ripe tomatoes, diced

handful of crisp lettuce
leaves, such as romaine or
iceberg, shredded

4–6 radishes, diced

3 scallions, thinly sliced

1 ripe avocado, pitted,
peeled, diced or sliced,
and tossed with lime juice

sour cream, to taste

1–2 canned chipotle chiles in
adobo marinade or dried
chipotle, reconstituted and
cut into thin strips

method

1 To make the tostadas, fry the tortillas in a small amount of oil in a nonstick skillet until crisp. Set aside.

2 Place the chicken in a pan with the stock and garlic. Bring to a boil, then reduce the heat and cook for 1–2 minutes, or until the chicken begins to turn opaque.

3 Remove the chicken from the heat and let stand in its hot liquid to cook through.

4 Heat the beans in a separate pan with enough water to form a smooth purée. Add the cumin and keep warm.

5 Reheat the tostadas under a preheated medium broiler, if necessary. Spread the hot beans on the tostadas, then sprinkle with the cheese. Lift the cooked chicken from the liquid and divide among the tostadas. Top with the cilantro, tomatoes, lettuce, radishes, scallions, avocado, sour cream, and a few strips of chipotle. Serve immediately.

chicken wraps

ingredients

SERVES 4

5 fl oz/150 ml/generous
   $^2/_3$ cup lowfat plain yogurt
1 tbsp whole-grain mustard
pepper
10 oz/280 g cooked skinless,
   boneless chicken
   breast, diced
5 oz/140 g iceberg lettuce,
   finely shredded
3 oz/85 g cucumber,
   thinly sliced
2 celery stalks, sliced
3 oz/85 g/$^1/_2$ cup black
   seedless grapes, halved
8 x 8-inch/20-cm soft flour
   tortillas or 4 x 10-inch/
   25-cm soft flour tortillas

method

1 Combine the yogurt and mustard in a bowl and season with pepper. Stir in the chicken and toss until thoroughly coated.

2 Put the lettuce, cucumber, celery, and grapes into a separate bowl and mix well.

3 Fold a tortilla in half and in half again to make a cone that is easy to hold. Half-fill the tortilla pocket with the salad mixture and top with some of the chicken mixture. Repeat with the remaining tortillas, salad, and chicken. Serve at once.

filo chicken pie

ingredients

SERVES 6–8

3 lb 5 oz/1.5 kg whole
  chicken
1 small onion, halved,
  and 3 large onions,
  chopped finely
1 carrot, sliced thickly
1 celery stalk, sliced thickly
pared zest of 1 lemon
1 bay leaf
10 peppercorns
5^1/$_2$ oz/155 g butter
2 oz/55 g/scant ^{1}/$_2$ cup
  all-purpose flour
5 fl oz/150 ml/^{2}/$_3$ cup milk
salt and pepper
1 oz/25 g/^{1}/$_3$ cup kefalotiri or
  romano cheese, grated
3 eggs, beaten
8 oz/225 g filo pastry (work
  with one sheet at a time
  and keep the remaining
  sheets covered with a
  damp dish towel)

method

1 Put the chicken in a large pan with the halved onion, carrot, celery, lemon zest, bay leaf, and peppercorns. Add cold water to cover and bring to a boil. Cover and simmer for about 1 hour, or until the chicken is cooked.

2 Remove the chicken and set aside to cool. Bring the stock to a boil and boil until reduced to about 20 fl oz/625 ml/2^1/$_2$ cups. Strain and reserve the stock. Cut the cooled chicken into bite-size pieces, discarding the skin and bones.

3 Fry the chopped onions until softened in 2 oz/55 g of the butter. Add the flour and cook gently, stirring, for 1–2 minutes. Gradually stir in the reserved stock and the milk. Bring to a boil, stirring constantly, then simmer for 1–2 minutes until thick and smooth. Remove from the heat, add the chicken, and season. Let cool, then stir in the cheese and eggs.

4 Melt the remaining butter and use a little to grease a deep 12 x 8-inch/30 x 20-cm metal baking pan. Cut the pastry sheets in half widthwise. Line the pan with one sheet of pastry and brush it with a little melted butter. Repeat with half of the pastry sheets. Spread the filling over the pastry, then top with the remaining pastry sheets, brushing each with butter and tucking down the edges.

5 Bake in a preheated oven, 375°F/190°C, for about 50 minutes, until golden. Serve warm.

green chile & chicken chilaquiles

ingredients

SERVES 4–6

12 stale tortillas, cut into
   strips
1 tbsp vegetable oil
1 small cooked chicken, meat
   removed from the bones
   and cut into bite-size
   pieces
salsa verde
3 tbsp chopped fresh cilantro
1 tsp finely chopped fresh
   oregano or thyme
4 garlic cloves, finely
   chopped
$1/4$ tsp ground cumin
12 oz/350 g/3 cups grated
   cheese, such as Cheddar,
   Manchego, or mozzarella
16 fl oz/500 ml/2 cups
   chicken stock
about 4 oz/115 g/$1^1/2$ cups
   freshly grated Parmesan
   cheese
12 fl oz/375 ml/$1^1/2$ cups
   sour cream
3–5 scallions, thinly sliced
pickled chiles, to serve

method

1 Place the tortilla strips in a roasting pan, toss with the oil and bake in a preheated oven, 375°F/190°C, for 30 minutes, or until they are crisp and golden.

2 Arrange the chicken pieces in a 9 x 13-inch/ 23 x 33-cm flameproof casserole, then sprinkle with half the salsa, cilantro, oregano, garlic, cumin, and some of the Cheddar, Manchego, or mozzarella cheese. Repeat these layers and top with the tortilla strips. Pour the stock over the top, then sprinkle with the remaining cheese.

3 Bake in the oven at the same temperature for 30 minutes, or until heated through and the cheese is lightly golden in some places.

4 Serve with a dollop of sour cream, sliced scallions, and pickled chiles.

pan-fried chicken & cilantro

ingredients

SERVES 4

1 bunch of fresh cilantro

1 tbsp corn oil

4 skinless, boneless chicken breasts, about 4 oz/115 g each, trimmed of all visible fat

1 tsp cornstarch

1 tbsp water

3 fl oz/90 ml/^{1}/$_3$ cup lowfat plain yogurt

2 tbsp reduced fat light cream

6 fl oz/175 ml/^{3}/$_4$ cup chicken stock

2 tbsp lime juice

2 garlic cloves, finely chopped

1 shallot, finely chopped

1 tomato, peeled, seeded, and chopped

salt and pepper

method

1 Set aside a few cilantro sprigs for a garnish and coarsely chop the remainder. Heat the corn oil in a heavy-bottom skillet, add the chicken and cook over medium heat for 5 minutes on each side, or until the juices run clear when the meat is pierced with the tip of a sharp knife. Remove from the skillet and keep warm.

2 Mix the cornstarch and water until smooth. Stir in the yogurt and cream. Pour the chicken stock and lime juice into the skillet and add the garlic and shallot. Reduce the heat and let simmer for 1 minute. Stir the tomato into the yogurt mixture and stir the mixture into the skillet. Season with salt and pepper. Cook, stirring constantly, for 1–2 minutes, or until slightly thickened, but do not let the mixture boil. Stir in the chopped fresh cilantro.

3 Place the chicken on a large serving plate, pour the sauce over it and garnish with the reserved cilantro sprigs. Serve.

...kabobs
...rt sauce

2 garlic cloves, crushed
juice of $1/2$ lemon
1 tbsp chopped fresh herbs
   such as oregano, dill,
   tarragon, or parsley
salt and pepper
4 large skinned, boned
   chicken breasts
oil, for oiling
8 firm stems of fresh
   rosemary, optional
shredded romaine lettuce,
   to serve
rice, to serve
lemon wedges, to garnish

method

1 To make the sauce, put the yogurt, garlic, lemon juice, herbs, salt, and pepper in a large bowl and mix well together.

2 Cut the chicken breasts into chunks measuring about $1^{1/2}$ inches/4 cm square. Add to the yogurt mixture and toss well together until the chicken pieces are coated. Cover and leave to marinate in the refrigerator for about 1 hour. If you are using wooden skewers, soak them in cold water for 30 minutes before use.

3 Preheat the broiler. Thread the pieces of chicken onto 8 flat, oiled, metal kabob skewers, wooden skewers, or rosemary stems and place on an oiled broiler pan.

4 Cook the kabobs under the broiler for about 15 minutes, turning and basting with the remaining marinade occasionally, until lightly browned and tender.

5 Pour the remaining marinade into a pan and heat gently but do not boil. Serve the kabobs with shredded lettuce on a bed of rice and garnish with lemon wedges. Accompany with the yogurt sauce.

gingered chicken kabobs

ingredients

SERVES 4

3 skinless, boneless chicken
    breasts, cut into small
    cubes

juice of 1 lime

1-inch/2.5-cm piece
    gingerroot, peeled and
    chopped

1 fresh red chile, seeded
    and sliced

2 tbsp vegetable or peanut oil

1 onion, sliced

2 garlic cloves, chopped

1 eggplant, cut into chunks

2 zucchini, cut into thick slices

1 red bell pepper, seeded and
    cut into squares

2 tbsp red curry paste

2 tbsp Thai soy sauce

1 tsp jaggery or soft light
    brown sugar

boiled rice, with chopped
    cilantro, to serve

method

1 Put the chicken cubes in a shallow dish. Mix the lime, gingerroot, and chile together and pour over the chicken pieces. Stir gently to coat. Cover and let chill in the refrigerator for at least 3 hours to marinate.

2 Soak 8–12 wooden skewers in cold water for 30 minutes before use, to prevent burning.

3 Thread the chicken pieces onto the soaked wooden skewers and cook under a hot broiler for 3–4 minutes, turning frequently, until they are cooked through.

4 Meanwhile, heat the oil in a wok or large skillet and sauté the onion and garlic for 1–2 minutes, until softened, but not browned. Add the eggplant, zucchini, and bell pepper and cook for 3–4 minutes, until cooked but still firm. Add the curry paste, soy sauce, and sugar, and cook for 1 minute.

5 Serve hot with boiled rice, stirred through with chopped cilantro.

thai-style chicken chunks

ingredients

SERVES 4

4 skinless, boneless chicken
breasts, cut into small
chunks

freshly cooked jasmine rice,
to serve

chopped fresh cilantro,
to garnish

marinade

1 red chile and 1 green chile,
seeded and finely
chopped

2 garlic cloves, chopped

1³/₄ oz/50 g chopped fresh
cilantro

1 tbsp finely chopped fresh
lemongrass

¹/₂ tsp ground turmeric

¹/₂ tsp garam masala

2 tsp brown sugar

2 tbsp Thai fish sauce

1 tbsp lime juice

salt and pepper

method

1 To make the marinade, put the red and
green chiles, garlic, cilantro, and lemongrass
into a food processor and process until
coarsely chopped. Add the turmeric, garam
masala, sugar, fish sauce, and lime juice,
season with salt and pepper, and blend until
smooth.

2 Put the chicken chunks into a nonmetallic
(glass or ceramic) bowl, which will not react
with acid. Pour over enough marinade to
cover the chicken, then cover with plastic
wrap and let chill for at least 2¹/₂ hours. Cover
the remaining marinade with plastic wrap and
let chill until the chicken is ready.

3 When the chicken chunks are thoroughly
marinated, lift them out, and grill them over
hot coals for 20 minutes, or until cooked right
through, turning them frequently and basting
with the remaining marinade. Arrange the
chicken on serving plates with some freshly
cooked jasmine rice. Garnish with chopped
fresh cilantro and serve.

grilled chicken with lemon

ingredients

SERVES 4

4 chicken fourths

grated rind and juice of
  2 lemons

4 tbsp olive oil

2 garlic cloves, crushed

2 sprigs fresh thyme, plus
  extra to garnish

salt and pepper

method

1 Prick the skin of the chicken fourths all over with a fork. Put the chicken pieces in a dish, add the lemon juice, oil, garlic, thyme, salt, and pepper, and mix well. Cover and let marinate in the refrigerator for at least 2 hours.

2 To cook the chicken, preheat the barbecue or broiler. Put the chicken on the barbecue grill or in a broiler pan and baste with the marinade. Cook for 30–40 minutes, basting and turning occasionally, until the chicken is tender. (To test if the chicken is cooked, pierce the thickest part of the chicken pieces with a skewer. If the juices run clear, it is ready.) Serve hot, garnished with thyme sprigs and the grated lemon rind.

hearty dishes

Although chicken is a light and easily digestible meat, chicken recipes can still be as robust and satisfying as you like. Start with a Traditional Roast Chicken, or Roasted Chicken with Sun-blush Tomato Pesto for a flavorful variation.

You will find favorite recipes from around the world in this chapter. From France come several classic dishes, including Coq au Vin and Provençal Chicken, both cooked in wine, one of the country's most famous commodities. From neighboring Italy comes Tuscan Chicken, while Chicken with Goat Cheese & Basil and Chicken with Walnut Sauce are Greek recipes.

Every meat has its ideal herb, and in the case of chicken, the herb is tarragon. Chicken with Tarragon has a delectable creamy sauce, with a hint of wine and garlic, too. For those who like a little more 'fire' in their flavorings, Red Hot Chile Chicken and Fiery Chicken Vindaloo really live up to their names.

If keeping your heart healthy is a major consideration, try Sticky Lime Chicken, Chicken with Saffron Mashed Potatoes, and Chicken Fricassée. If you are diabetic, Roast Cinnamon Squab Chickens with Spiced Lentils and Spanish Chicken with Preserved Lemons are two recipes especially for you.

traditional roast chicken

ingredients

SERVES 4

1 oz/25 g butter, softened

1 garlic clove,
    finely chopped

3 tbsp finely chopped
    toasted walnuts

1 tbsp chopped
    fresh parsley

salt and pepper

1 oven-ready chicken,
    weighing 4 lb/1.8 kg

1 lime, cut into fourths

2 tbsp vegetable oil

1 tbsp cornstarch

2 tbsp water

lime wedges and fresh
    rosemary sprigs,
    to garnish

roast potatoes and a selection
    of freshly cooked
    vegetables, to serve

method

1 Mix 1 tablespoon of the butter with the garlic, walnuts, and parsley together in a small bowl. Season well with salt and pepper. Loosen the skin from the breast of the chicken without breaking it. Spread the butter mixture evenly between the skin and breast meat. Place the lime fourths inside the body cavity.

2 Pour the oil into a roasting pan. Transfer the chicken to the pan and dot the skin with the remaining butter. Roast in a preheated oven, 375°F/190°C, for 1¾ hours, basting occasionally, until the chicken is tender and the juices run clear when a skewer is inserted into the thickest part of the meat. Lift out the chicken and place on a serving platter to rest for 10 minutes.

3 Blend the cornstarch with the water, then stir into the juices in the pan. Stir over low heat until thickened, adding more water if necessary. Garnish the chicken with lime wedges and rosemary sprigs. Serve with roast potatoes and a selection of freshly cooked vegetables and spoon over the thickened juices.

roasted chicken with sun-blush tomato pesto

ingredients

SERVES 4

4 skinless, boneless chicken
breasts, about 1 lb 12 oz/
800 g in total
1 tbsp olive oil
salt and pepper
2 tbsp pine nuts, lightly
toasted, to garnish

pesto

$4^1/2$ oz/125 g sun-blush
tomatoes in oil (drained
weight), chopped
2 garlic cloves, crushed
4 tbsp pine nuts,
lightly toasted
5 fl oz/150 ml/$^2/_3$ cup extra-
virgin olive oil

method

1 To make the red pesto, put the sun-blush tomatoes, garlic, 4 tablespoons of the pine nuts, and oil into a food processor and process to a coarse paste.

2 Arrange the chicken in a large, ovenproof dish or roasting pan. Brush each breast with the oil, then place a tablespoon of red pesto over each breast. Using the back of a spoon, spread the pesto so that it covers the top of each breast. (Store the remaining pesto in an airtight container in the refrigerator for up to 1 week.)

3 Roast the chicken in a preheated oven, 400°F/200°C for 30 minutes, or until tender and the juices run clear when a skewer is inserted into the thickest part of the meat.

4 Serve sprinkled with toasted pine nuts.

sticky lime chicken

ingredients

SERVES 4

4 part-boned, skinless
  chicken breasts, about
  5 oz/140 g each
grated rind and juice of 1 lime
1 tbsp honey
1 tbsp olive oil
1 garlic clove, chopped
  (optional)
1 tbsp chopped fresh thyme
pepper
boiled new potatoes and
  lightly cooked seasonal
  vegetables, to serve

method

1 Arrange the chicken breasts in a shallow roasting pan.

2 Put the lime rind and juice, honey, oil, garlic, if using, and thyme in a small bowl and combine thoroughly. Spoon the mixture evenly over the chicken breasts and season with pepper.

3 Roast the chicken in a preheated oven, 375°F/190°C, basting every 10 minutes, for 35–40 minutes, or until the chicken is tender and the juices run clear when a skewer is inserted into the thickest part of the meat. If the juices still run pink, return the chicken to the oven and cook for an additional 5 minutes, then test again. As the chicken cooks, the liquid in the pan thickens to give a tasty, sticky coating.

4 Serve with boiled new potatoes and lightly cooked seasonal vegetables.

roast cinnamon squab chickens with lentils

ingredients

SERVES 4

4 squab chickens, about
   1 lb 2 oz/500 g each

2 tbsp maple syrup

1 tsp ground cinnamon

1 tbsp vegetable oil

3$^1\!/_2$ fl oz/100 ml/generous $^1\!/_3$
   cup low-salt chicken stock

2 red onions, sliced

1 tsp cumin seeds

1 tsp coriander seeds

1 tbsp olive oil

2 garlic cloves, crushed

1 lb 12 oz/800 g canned
   lentils, drained and rinsed

1 tbsp unsalted butter

2 tbsp chopped fresh parsley

pepper

steamed broccoli or green
   beans, to serve

method

1 Arrange the squab chickens in a roasting pan. Mix the maple syrup, cinnamon, and vegetable oil together in a small bowl and brush over the breasts of the squab chickens. Pour the stock into the roasting pan and tuck the onion slices around the birds. Roast in a preheated oven, 375°F/190°C, for 35 minutes.

2 Meanwhile, heat a nonstick skillet over medium heat, add the cumin and coriander seeds, and cook, turning, until they start to give off an aroma. Tip into a mortar and finely crush with a pestle.

3 Heat the olive oil in a skillet over low heat, add the garlic and spices, and cook for 1–2 minutes, stirring constantly. Add the lentils and cook for 10–15 minutes, stirring occasionally.

4 When the birds are cooked, remove from the oven, transfer to a warmed plate, and keep warm. Put the roasting pan on the stove and bring the cooking juices up to a simmer. Stir in the butter and half the parsley. Season with pepper.

5 To serve, divide the lentils among 4 warmed serving plates. Add a squab chicken to each plate, pour over the sauce, and sprinkle with the remaining parsley. Serve with steamed broccoli or green beans.

chicken with saffron mash potatoes

ingredients

SERVES 4

1 lb 4 oz/550 g mealy
potatoes, cut into chunks
1 garlic clove, peeled
1 tsp saffron threads, crushed
40 fl oz/1.25 liters/5 cups
chicken or
vegetable stock
4 skinless, boneless chicken
breasts, trimmed of all
visible fat
2 tbsp olive oil
1 tbsp lemon juice
1 tbsp chopped fresh thyme
1 tbsp chopped fresh cilantro
1 tbsp coriander seeds, crushed
3½ fl oz/100 ml/⅓ cup
hot skim milk
salt and pepper
fresh thyme sprigs, to garnish

method

1 Put the potatoes, garlic, and saffron in a large heavy-bottom pan, add the stock and bring to a boil. Cover and let simmer for 20 minutes, or until tender.

2 Meanwhile, brush the chicken breasts all over with half the olive oil and all of the lemon juice. Sprinkle with the fresh thyme, cilantro, and the crushed coriander seeds. Heat a griddle pan, add the chicken, and cook over medium-high heat for 5 minutes on each side, or until the juices run clear when the meat is pierced with the tip of a sharp knife. Alternatively, cook the chicken breasts under a preheated medium-hot broiler for 5 minutes on each side, or until cooked through.

3 Drain the potatoes and return the contents of the strainer to the pan. Add the remaining olive oil and the milk, season with salt and pepper, and mash until smooth. Divide the saffron mash among 4 large, warmed serving plates, top with a piece of chicken, and garnish with a few sprigs of fresh thyme. Serve.

tarragon chicken

ingredients

SERVES 4

4 skinless, boneless chicken
    breasts, about 6 oz/
    175 g each
salt and pepper
4 fl oz/125 ml/^{1}/$_2$ cup
    dry white wine
8–10 fl oz/250–300 ml/
    1–1^1/$_4$ cups chicken stock
1 garlic clove, finely chopped
1 tbsp dried tarragon
6 fl oz/175 ml/^{3}/$_4$ cup
    heavy cream
1 tbsp chopped fresh tarragon
fresh tarragon sprigs,
    to garnish

method

1 Season the chicken with salt and pepper and place in a single layer in a large, heavy-bottom skillet. Pour in the wine and just enough chicken stock to cover, and add the garlic and dried tarragon. Bring to a boil, reduce the heat, and cook gently for 10 minutes, or until the chicken is tender and cooked through.

2 Remove the chicken with a slotted spoon or tongs, cover, and keep warm. Strain the poaching liquid into a clean skillet and skim off any fat from the surface. Bring to a boil and cook for 12–15 minutes, or until reduced by about two-thirds.

3 Stir in the cream, return to a boil, and cook until reduced by about half. Stir in the fresh tarragon. Slice the chicken breasts and arrange on warmed plates. Spoon over the sauce, garnish with tarragon sprigs, and serve immediately.

icken

3 tbsp

1 red onion, chopped

2 garlic cloves, chopped finely

1 red bell pepper, seeded and
    chopped

pinch of saffron threads

5 fl oz/150 ml/⅔ cup chicken
    stock or a mixture of
    chicken stock and dry
    white wine

14 oz/400 g canned
    tomatoes, chopped

4 sun-dried tomatoes in oil,
    drained and chopped

8 oz/225 g portobello
    mushrooms, sliced

4 oz/115 g/⅔ cup black
    olives, pitted

4 tbsp lemon juice

fresh basil leaves, to garnish

tagliatelle, fettuccine, or
    tagliarini and crusty bread,
    to serve

method

1 Place the flour on a shallow plate and season with salt and pepper. Coat the chicken in the seasoned flour, shaking off any excess. Heat the olive oil in a large, flameproof casserole. Add the chicken and cook over medium heat, turning frequently, for 5–7 minutes, until golden brown. Remove from the casserole and set aside.

2 Add the onion, garlic, and red bell pepper to the casserole, reduce the heat and cook, stirring occasionally, for 5 minutes, until softened. Meanwhile, stir the saffron into the stock.

3 Stir the tomatoes, with the juice from the can, and the sun-dried tomatoes, mushrooms, and olives into the casserole and cook, stirring occasionally, for 3 minutes. Pour in the stock and saffron mixture and the lemon juice. Bring to a boil, then return the chicken to the casserole.

4 Cover and cook in a preheated oven, 350°F/ 180°C, for 1 hour, until the chicken is tender. Garnish with the basil leaves and serve immediately with pasta and crusty bread.

pesto & ricotta chicken

ingredients

SERVES 4

1 tbsp pesto sauce

4 oz/115 g/^{1}/$_2$ cup ricotta
    cheese

4 x 6-oz/175-g skinless,
    boneless chicken breasts

1 tbsp olive oil

pepper

small salad, to garnish

tomato vinaigrette

3^1/$_2$ fl oz/100 ml/generous
    ^{1}/$_3$ cup olive oil

1 bunch fresh chives

1 lb 2 oz/500 g tomatoes,
    peeled, seeded,
    and chopped

juice and finely grated rind
    of 1 lime

salt and pepper

method

1 Mix together the pesto and ricotta in a small bowl until well combined. Using a sharp knife, cut a deep slit in the side of each chicken breast to make a pocket. Spoon the ricotta mixture into the pockets and reshape the chicken breasts to enclose it. Place the chicken on a plate, cover, and let chill for 30 minutes.

2 To make the vinaigrette, pour the olive oil into a blender or food processor, add the chives, and process until smooth. Scrape the mixture into a bowl and stir in the tomatoes, lime juice, and lime rind. Season with salt and pepper.

3 Brush the chicken with the olive oil and season with pepper. Grill on a fairly hot barbecue for about 8 minutes on each side, or until cooked through and tender. Transfer to serving plates, spoon over the vinaigrette, and serve at once.

chicken rolls with cheese & pine kernels

ingredients

SERVES 6

3 slices white bread, crusts removed

6 skinless, boneless chicken breasts, about 6 oz/ 175 g each

2 shallots, finely chopped

2 garlic cloves, finely chopped

2 tbsp finely chopped fresh flat-leaf parsley

2 tbsp freshly grated Parmesan cheese

2 oz/55 g/$\frac{1}{3}$ cup pine nuts

pinch of ground mace

salt and pepper

tarragon-flavored oil or olive oil, for brushing

few sprigs of fresh flat-leaf parsley, to garnish

method

1 Tear the bread into pieces, place in a bowl, and add cold water to cover. Set aside to soak for 10 minutes.

2 Meanwhile, place the chicken breasts between 2 sheets of plastic wrap and pound gently with a meat mallet or the side of a rolling pin to flatten.

3 Drain the bread and squeeze out the excess liquid. Mix together the bread, shallots, garlic, parsley, Parmesan, pine nuts, and mace in a bowl. Season with salt and pepper.

4 Spread the filling evenly over the chicken breasts and roll up. Secure each roll with a wooden toothpick. Brush with the oil and grill, turning frequently and brushing with more oil as necessary, for 25–30 minutes, or until cooked through and tender. Serve at once, garnished with parsley.

chicken with goat cheese & basil

ingredients

SERVES 4

4 skinned chicken breast fillets

3$^1/_2$ oz/100 g soft goat cheese

small bunch fresh basil

salt and pepper

2 tbsp olive oil

method

1 Using a sharp knife, slit along one long edge of each chicken breast, then carefully open out each breast to make a small pocket. Divide the cheese equally among the pockets, and tuck three or four basil leaves in each. Close the openings and season the breasts with salt and pepper.

2 Heat the oil in a skillet, add the chicken breasts, and fry gently for 15–20 minutes, turning several times, until golden and tender.

3 Serve warm, garnished with a sprig of basil.

chicken with walnut sauce

ingredients

SERVES 4

4–8 skinned chicken pieces

$1/2$ lemon, cut into wedges

3 tbsp olive oil

5 fl oz/150 ml/$2/3$ cup dry white wine

10 fl oz/300 ml/$1 1/4$ cups chicken stock

1 bay leaf

salt and pepper

$3 1/2$ oz/100 g/$3/4$ cup walnut pieces

2 garlic cloves

5 fl oz/150 ml/$2/3$ cup strained plain yogurt

chopped fresh flat-leaf parsley, to garnish

rice or pilaf and pita bread, to serve

method

1 Rub the chicken pieces with the lemon. Heat the oil in a large skillet, add the chicken pieces, and fry quickly until lightly browned on all sides.

2 Pour the wine into the skillet and bring to a boil. Add the stock, bay leaf, salt, and pepper and simmer for about 20 minutes, turning several times, until the chicken is tender.

3 Meanwhile, put the walnuts and garlic in a food processor and blend to form a fairly smooth purée.

4 When the chicken is cooked, transfer to a warmed serving dish and keep warm. Stir the walnut mixture and yogurt into the pan juices and heat gently for about 5 minutes until the sauce is quite thick. (Do not boil or the sauce will curdle.) Season with salt and pepper.

5 Pour the walnut sauce over the chicken pieces and serve hot with rice, or pilaf, and pita bread. Garnish with chopped fresh parsley.

chicken tagine

ingredients

SERVES 4

1 tbsp olive oil

1 onion, cut into small wedges

2–4 garlic cloves, sliced

1 lb/450 g skinless, boneless
chicken breast, diced

1 tsp ground cumin

2 cinnamon sticks, lightly
bruised

1 tbsp all-purpose
whole wheat flour

8 oz/225 g eggplant, diced

1 red bell pepper, seeded and
chopped

3 oz/85 g white mushrooms,
sliced

1 tbsp tomato paste

20 fl oz/625 ml/2^1/$_2$ cups
chicken stock

10 oz/280 g canned chickpeas,
drained and rinsed

2 oz/55 g/^{1}/$_3$ cup no-soak
dried apricots, chopped

salt and pepper

1 tbsp chopped fresh cilantro

method

1 Heat the oil in a large pan over medium heat, add the onion and garlic, and cook for 3 minutes, stirring frequently. Add the chicken and cook, stirring constantly, for an additional 5 minutes, or until sealed on all sides. Add the cumin and cinnamon sticks to the pan halfway through sealing the chicken.

2 Sprinkle in the flour and cook, stirring constantly, for 2 minutes. Add the eggplant, red bell pepper, and mushrooms and cook for an additional 2 minutes, stirring constantly.

3 Blend the tomato paste with the stock, stir into the pan, and bring to a boil. Reduce the heat and add the chickpeas and apricots. Cover and let simmer for 15–20 minutes, or until the chicken is tender.

4 Season with salt and pepper and serve at once, sprinkled with cilantro.

chicken kiev

ingredients

SERVES 4

4 tbsp butter, softened

1 garlic clove, finely chopped

1 tbsp finely chopped fresh
parsley

1 tbsp finely chopped fresh
oregano

salt and pepper

4 skinless, boneless chicken
breasts

3 oz/85 g fresh white or
whole wheat bread
crumbs

3 tbsp freshly grated
Parmesan cheese

1 egg, beaten

9 fl oz/250 ml vegetable oil,
for deep-frying

slices of lemon and flat-leaf
parsley sprigs, to garnish

freshly cooked new potatoes
and selection of cooked
vegetables, to serve

method

1 Place the butter and garlic in a bowl and mix together well. Stir in the chopped herbs and season well with salt and pepper. Pound the chicken breasts to flatten them to an even thickness, then place a tablespoon of herb butter in the center of each one. Fold in the sides to enclose the butter, then secure with wooden toothpicks.

2 Combine the bread crumbs and grated Parmesan on a plate. Dip the chicken parcels into the beaten egg, then coat in the bread crumb mixture. Transfer to a plate, cover, and let chill for 30 minutes. Remove from the refrigerator and coat in the egg and then the breadcrumb mixture for a second time.

3 Pour the oil into a deep-fryer to a depth that will cover the chicken parcels. Heat until it reaches 350–375°F/180–190°C, or until a cube of bread browns in 30 seconds. Transfer the chicken to the hot oil and deep-fry for 5 minutes, or until cooked through. Lift out the chicken and drain on paper towels.

4 Divide the chicken among 4 serving plates, garnish with lemon slices and parsley sprigs, and serve with new potatoes and a selection of vegetables.

chicken fricassée

ingredients

SERVES 4

1 tbsp all-purpose flour

salt and white pepper

4 skinless, boneless chicken
breasts, about 5 oz/140 g
each, trimmed of all visible
fat and cut into ³/₄-inch/
2-cm cubes

1 tbsp sunflower or corn oil

8 pearl onions

2 garlic cloves, crushed

8 fl oz/250 ml/1 cup
chicken stock

2 carrots, diced

2 celery stalks, diced

8 oz/225 g/2 cups
frozen peas

1 yellow bell pepper, seeded
and diced

4 oz/115 g white mushrooms,
sliced

4 fl oz/125 ml/¹/₂ cup lowfat
plain yogurt

3 tbsp chopped fresh parsley

method

1 Spread out the flour on a dish and season with salt and pepper. Add the chicken and, using your hands, coat in the flour. Heat the oil in a heavy-bottom pan. Add the onions and garlic and cook over low heat, stirring occasionally, for 5 minutes. Add the chicken and cook, stirring, for 10 minutes, or until just beginning to color.

2 Gradually stir in the stock, then add the carrots, celery, and peas. Bring to a boil, then reduce the heat, cover, and let simmer for 5 minutes. Add the bell pepper and mushrooms, cover, and let simmer for an additional 10 minutes.

3 Stir in the yogurt and chopped parsley and season with salt and pepper. Cook for 1–2 minutes, or until heated through, then transfer to 4 large, warmed serving plates and serve immediately.

provençal chicken

ingredients

SERVES 4

4 lb/1.8 kg chicken pieces

salt and pepper

1 garlic clove, finely chopped

3 tbsp olive oil

1 onion, finely chopped

8 oz/225 g mushrooms, halved

1 tbsp all-purpose flour

4 fl oz/125 ml/^{1}/$_2$ cup
   chicken stock

6 fl oz/175 ml/^{3}/$_4$ cup
   dry white wine

6 canned anchovy fillets,
   drained

3 tomatoes, peeled, seeded
   and chopped

2 tsp chopped fresh oregano

6 black olives, pitted

method

1 Rub the chicken pieces all over with salt, pepper, and garlic. Heat the oil in a flameproof casserole. Add the chicken and cook over medium heat, turning occasionally, for 8–10 minutes, or until golden. Add the onion, cover, and cook over low heat, stirring occasionally, for 20–25 minutes, or until cooked through and tender.

2 Transfer the chicken to a large serving plate, cover, and keep warm. Add the mushrooms to the casserole and cook over medium heat, stirring constantly, for 3 minutes. Add the flour and cook, stirring constantly, for 1 minute, then gradually stir in the stock and wine. Bring to a boil and cook, stirring, for 10 minutes, or until thickened.

3 Coarsely chop 4 of the anchovies and add them to the casserole with the tomatoes, oregano, and olives, then let simmer for 5 minutes. Meanwhile, cut the remaining anchovies in half lengthwise. Transfer the sauce and chicken to serving plates, garnish with the halved anchovies, and serve immediately.

coq au vin

ingredients

SERVES 4

2 tbsp butter

8 baby onions

4^1/$_2$ oz/125 g bacon,
    roughly chopped

4 chicken joints

1 garlic clove, finely chopped

12 white mushrooms

10 fl oz/300 ml/1^1/$_4$ cups red
    wine

bouquet garni sachet

1 tbsp chopped fresh tarragon

salt and pepper

2 tsp cornstarch

1–2 tbsp cold water

fresh flat-leaf parsley
    sprigs, to garnish

sautéed sliced potatoes,
    to serve

method

1 Melt half of the butter in a large skillet over medium heat. Add the onions and bacon and cook, stirring, for 3 minutes. Lift out the bacon and onions and reserve.

2 Melt the remaining butter in the skillet and add the chicken joints. Cook for 3 minutes, then turn over and cook on the other side for 2 minutes. Drain off some of the chicken fat, then return the bacon and onions to the pan. Add the garlic, mushrooms, red wine, bouquet garni, and tarragon. Season with salt and pepper. Cook for about 1 hour, or until the chicken is cooked through.

3 Remove the skillet from the heat, lift out the chicken, onions, bacon, and mushrooms, transfer them to a serving platter, and keep warm. Discard the bouquet garni.

4 Mix the cornstarch with enough of the water to make a paste, then stir into the juices in the skillet. Bring to a boil, reduce the heat, and cook, stirring, for 1 minute. Pour the sauce over the chicken, garnish with parsley sprigs, and serve with sautéed sliced potatoes.

spanish chicken with preserved lemons

ingredients

SERVES 4

1 tbsp all-purpose flour

4 chicken quarters, skin on

2 tbsp olive oil

2 garlic cloves, crushed

1 large Spanish onion, thinly
    sliced

24 fl oz/750 ml/3 cups
    low-salt chicken stock

$1/2$ tsp saffron threads

2 yellow bell peppers, seeded
    and cut into chunks

2 preserved lemons, cut into
    fourths

9 oz/250 g/generous $1^{1}/4$
    cups brown basmati rice

white pepper

12 pimiento-stuffed green
    olives

chopped fresh parsley,
    to garnish

salad greens, to serve

method

1 Put the flour into a large freezer bag. Add the chicken, close the top of the bag, and shake to coat with flour.

2 Heat the oil in a large skillet over low heat, add the garlic, and cook for 1 minute, stirring constantly. Add the chicken to the skillet and cook over medium heat, turning frequently, for 5 minutes, or until the skin has lightly browned, then remove to a plate. Add the onion to the skillet and cook, stirring occasionally, for 10 minutes until soft.

3 Meanwhile, put the stock and saffron into a pan over low heat and heat through.

4 Transfer the chicken and onion to a large casserole dish, add the yellow bell peppers, lemons, and rice, then pour over the stock. Mix well and season with pepper.

5 Cover and cook in a preheated oven, 350°F/180°C, for 50 minutes, or until the chicken is cooked through and tender. Reduce the oven temperature to 325°F/160°C. Add the olives to the casserole and cook for an additional 10 minutes.

6 Serve sprinkled with chopped parsley and accompanied by salad greens.

chicken with yucatan vinegar sauce

ingredients

SERVES 4–6

8 small boned chicken thighs

chicken stock

15–20 garlic cloves, unpeeled

1 tsp coarsely ground
   black pepper

$^1/_2$ tsp ground cloves

2 tsp crumbled dried oregano
   or $^1/_2$ tsp crushed
   bay leaves

about $^1/_2$ tsp salt

1 tbsp lime juice

1 tsp cumin seeds, lightly
   toasted

1 tbsp all-purpose flour, plus
   extra for dredging

4 fl oz/125ml/$^1/_2$ cup
   vegetable oil

3–4 onions, thinly sliced

2 fresh chiles, preferably mild
   yellow ones, such as
   Mexican Guero or similar
   Turkish or Greek chiles,
   seeded and sliced

3$^1/_2$ fl oz/100 ml/generous
   $^1/_3$ cup cider vinegar or
   sherry vinegar

method

1 Place the chicken in a pan with enough stock to cover. Bring to a boil, then reduce the heat and let simmer for 5 minutes. Remove from the heat and let cool in the stock.

2 Meanwhile, roast the garlic in an unoiled skillet until the cloves are lightly browned on all sides and tender inside. Remove from the heat. Let cool, then squeeze the flesh from the skins into a bowl. Using a mortar and pestle, grind the garlic with the pepper, cloves, oregano, salt, lime juice, and three-fourths of the cumin seeds. Mix with the flour.

3 Remove the chicken from the stock, reserving the stock, and pat dry. Rub with two-thirds of the spice paste. Cover and let stand at room temperature for at least 30 minutes.

4 Heat a little of the oil in a skillet and cook the onions and chiles until golden brown and softened. Pour in the vinegar and remaining cumin seeds, cook for a few minutes, then add the reserved stock and remaining spice paste. Boil, stirring, until reduced in volume.

5 Dredge the chicken in flour. Heat the remaining oil in a heavy-bottom skillet. Fry the chicken until lightly browned and the juices run clear when a skewer is inserted into the thickest part. Serve topped with the sauce.

louisiana chicken

ingredients

SERVES 4

5 tbsp corn oil

4 chicken portions

6 tbsp all-purpose flour

1 onion, chopped

2 celery stalks, sliced

1 green bell pepper, seeded
    and chopped

2 garlic cloves, finely
    chopped

2 tsp chopped fresh thyme

2 fresh red chiles, seeded
    and finely chopped

14 oz/400 g canned
    chopped tomatoes

10 fl oz/300 ml/1¼ cups
    chicken stock

salt and pepper

corn salad and chopped
    fresh thyme, to garnish

method

1 Heat the oil in a large, heavy-bottomed pan or flameproof casserole. Add the chicken and cook over medium heat, stirring, for 5–10 minutes, or until golden. Transfer the chicken to a plate with a perforated spoon.

2 Stir the flour into the oil and cook over very low heat, stirring constantly, for 15 minutes, or until light golden. Do not let it burn. Add the onion, celery, and green bell pepper and cook, stirring constantly, for 2 minutes. Add the garlic, thyme, and chiles and cook, stirring, for 1 minute.

3 Stir in the tomatoes and their juices, then gradually stir in the stock. Return the chicken pieces to the pan, cover, and simmer for 45 minutes, or until the chicken is cooked through and tender. Season with salt and pepper, transfer to warmed serving plates and serve immediately, garnished with some corn salad and a sprinkling of chopped thyme.

red hot chili chicken

ingredients

SERVES 4

1 tbsp curry paste

2 fresh green chiles, chopped

5 dried red chiles

2 tbsp tomato paste

2 garlic cloves, chopped

1 tsp chili powder

pinch of sugar

pinch of salt

2 tbsp peanut or corn oil

$1/2$ tsp cumin seeds

1 onion, chopped

2 curry leaves

1 tsp ground cumin

1 tsp ground coriander

$1/2$ tsp ground turmeric

14 oz/400 g canned chopped
   tomatoes

5 fl oz/150 ml/$2/3$ cup
   chicken stock

4 skinless, boneless chicken
   breasts

1 tsp garam masala

freshly cooked rice and plain
   yogurt, to serve

method

1 To make the chili paste, place the curry paste, fresh and dried chiles, tomato paste, garlic, chili powder, and sugar in a blender or food processor with the salt. Process to a smooth paste.

2 Heat the oil in a large, heavy-bottom pan. Add the cumin seeds and cook over medium heat, stirring constantly, for 2 minutes, or until they begin to pop and release their aroma. Add the onion and curry leaves and cook, stirring, for 5 minutes.

3 Add the chili paste, cook for 2 minutes, then stir in the ground cumin, coriander, and turmeric and cook for an additional 2 minutes.

4 Add the tomatoes and their juices and the stock. Bring to a boil, then reduce the heat and simmer for 5 minutes. Add the chicken and garam masala, cover, and simmer gently for 20 minutes, or until the chicken is cooked through and tender. Serve immediately with freshly cooked rice and yogurt.

chicken & peanut curry

ingredients

SERVES 4

1 tbsp vegetable or peanut oil

2 red onions, sliced

2 tbsp Penang curry paste

14 fl oz/425 ml/1³/₄ cups
    coconut milk

5 fl oz/150 ml/²/₃ cup
    chicken stock

4 kaffir lime leaves, torn
    coarsely

1 lemongrass stalk, chopped
    finely

6 skinless, boneless chicken
    thighs, chopped

1 tbsp fish sauce

2 tbsp Thai soy sauce

1 tsp jaggery or soft, light
    brown sugar

1³/₄ oz/50 g/¹/₂ cup unsalted
    peanuts, roasted and
    chopped, plus extra
    to garnish

6 oz/175 g fresh pineapple,
    chopped coarsely

6-inch/15-cm piece
    cucumber, peeled,
    seeded, and sliced thickly,
    plus extra to garnish

method

1 Heat the oil in a wok and stir-fry the onions for 1 minute. Add the curry paste and stir-fry for 1–2 minutes.

2 Pour in the coconut milk and stock. Add the lime leaves and lemongrass and let simmer for 1 minute. Add the chicken and gradually bring to a boil. Let simmer for 8–10 minutes, until the chicken is tender.

3 Stir in the fish sauce, soy sauce, and sugar, and let simmer for 1–2 minutes. Stir in the peanuts, pineapple, and cucumber, and cook for 30 seconds. Serve immediately, sprinkled with the extra nuts and cucumber.

thai red chicken curry

ingredients

SERVES 4

6 garlic cloves, chopped

2 fresh red chiles, chopped

2 tbsp chopped fresh
   lemongrass

1 tsp finely grated lime rind

1 tbsp chopped fresh kaffir
   lime leaves

1 tbsp Thai red curry paste

1 tbsp coriander seeds,
   toasted and crushed

1 tbsp chili oil

4 skinless, boneless chicken
   breasts, sliced

10 fl oz/300 ml/1^1/4 cups
   coconut milk

10 fl oz/300 ml/1^1/4 cups
   chicken stock

1 tbsp soy sauce

2 oz/55 g/^{1}/3 cup shelled
   unsalted peanuts,
   toasted and ground

3 scallions,
   diagonally sliced

1 red bell pepper, seeded
   and sliced

3 Thai eggplants, sliced

2 tbsp chopped fresh Thai
   basil or fresh cilantro

fresh cilantro, to garnish

freshly cooked jasmine rice,
   to serve

method

1 Place the garlic, chiles, lemongrass, lime rind, lime leaves, curry paste, and coriander seeds in a food processor and process until the mixture is smooth.

2 Heat the oil in a preheated wok or large skillet over high heat. Add the chicken and the garlic mixture and stir-fry for 5 minutes. Add the coconut milk, stock, and soy sauce and bring to a boil. Reduce the heat and cook, stirring, for an additional 3 minutes. Stir in the ground peanuts and let simmer for 20 minutes.

3 Add the scallions, bell pepper, and eggplants and let simmer, stirring occasionally, for an additional 10 minutes. Remove from the heat, stir in the basil, and garnish with cilantro. Serve immediately with freshly cooked jasmine rice.

green chicken curry

ingredients

SERVES 4

1 tbsp vegetable or peanut oil

1 onion, sliced

1 garlic clove, chopped finely

2–3 tbsp green curry paste

14 fl oz/425 ml/1³/₄ cups
   coconut milk

5 fl oz/150 ml/²/₃ cup
   chicken stock

4 kaffir lime leaves

4 skinless, boneless chicken
   breasts, cut into cubes

1 tbsp fish sauce

2 tbsp Thai soy sauce

grated rind and juice of
   ¹/₂ lime

1 tsp jaggery or soft light
   brown sugar

4 tbsp chopped fresh cilantro,
   to garnish

freshly cooked rice, to serve

method

1 Heat the oil in a wok or large skillet and stir-fry the onion and garlic for 1–2 minutes, until starting to soften. Add the curry paste and stir-fry for 1–2 minutes.

2 Add the coconut milk, stock, and lime leaves, bring to a boil and add the chicken. Reduce the heat and let simmer gently for 15–20 minutes, until the chicken is tender.

3 Add the fish sauce, soy sauce, lime rind and juice, and sugar. Cook for 2–3 minutes, until the sugar has dissolved. Garnish with chopped cilantro and serve immediately, with rice.

fiery chicken vindaloo

ingredients

SERVES 4

1 tsp ground cumin

1 tsp ground cinnamon

2 tsp mustard powder

1 tsp ground coriander

1 tsp cayenne pepper

5 tbsp red wine vinegar

1 tsp brown sugar

$2/3$ cup vegetable oil

8 garlic cloves, crushed

3 red onions, sliced

4 skinless chicken breasts,
   cut into bite-size chunks

2 small red chiles, seeded
   and chopped

1 lb/450 g potatoes, peeled
   and chopped

1 lb 12 oz/800 g canned
   chopped tomatoes

1 tbsp tomato paste

a few drops of red
   food coloring

salt and pepper

freshly boiled rice, to serve

method

1 Put the cumin, cinnamon, mustard, coriander, and cayenne pepper into a bowl. Add the vinegar and sugar and mix well.

2 Heat the oil in a large skillet. Add the garlic and onions and cook, stirring, over medium heat for 5 minutes. Add the chicken and cook for another 3 minutes, then add the chiles, potatoes, chopped tomatoes and tomato paste, and a few drops of red food coloring. Stir in the spice mixture, season generously with salt and pepper, and bring to a boil. Lower the heat, cover the pan, and let simmer, stirring occasionally, for 1 hour.

3 Arrange the cooked rice on a large serving platter. Remove the pan from the heat, spoon the chicken mixture over the rice, and serve.

chicken pasanda

ingredients

SERVES 4

4 cardamom pods

6 black peppercorns

1/2 cinnamon stick

1/2 tsp cumin seeds

2 tsp garam masala

1 tsp chili powder

1 tsp grated fresh gingerroot

1 garlic clove, very finely
    chopped

4 tbsp thick plain yogurt

pinch of salt

1 lb 8 oz/675 g skinless,
    boneless chicken, diced

5 tbsp peanut oil

2 onions, finely chopped

3 fresh green chiles, seeded
    and chopped

2 tbsp chopped fresh cilantro

4 fl oz/125 ml/1/2 cup
    light cream

fresh cilantro sprigs,
    to garnish

method

1 Place the cardamom pods in a nonmetallic dish with the peppercorns, cinnamon, cumin, garam masala, chili powder, gingerroot, garlic, yogurt, and salt. Add the chicken pieces and stir well to coat. Cover and let marinate in the refrigerator for 2–3 hours.

2 Heat the oil in a preheated wok. Add the onions and cook over low heat, stirring occasionally, for 5 minutes, or until softened, then add the chicken pieces and marinade and cook over medium heat, stirring, for 15 minutes, or until the chicken is cooked through.

3 Stir in the fresh chiles and cilantro and pour in the cream. Heat through gently, but do not let it boil. Garnish with fresh cilantro and serve immediately.

gong bau chicken

ingredients

SERVES 4

2 boneless chicken breasts, with or without skin, cut into $^1/_2$-inch/1-cm cubes

1 tbsp vegetable or peanut oil

10 dried red chiles or more, to taste, snipped into 2 or 3 pieces

1 tsp Sichuan peppers

3 garlic cloves, finely sliced

1-inch/2.5-cm piece of fresh gingerroot, finely sliced

1 tbsp coarsely chopped scallion, white part only

3 oz/85 g/generous $^1/_2$ cup peanuts, roasted

marinade

2 tsp light soy sauce

1 tsp Shaoxing rice wine

$^1/_2$ tsp sugar

sauce

1 tsp light soy sauce

1 tsp dark soy sauce

1 tsp black Chinese rice vinegar

a few drops of sesame oil

2 tbsp chicken stock

1 tsp sugar

method

1 Combine all the ingredients for the marinade in a bowl and marinate the chicken, covered, for at least 20 minutes. Mix together all the ingredients for the sauce and set aside.

2 In a preheated wok or deep pan, heat the oil and stir-fry the chiles and peppers until crisp and fragrant. Toss in the chicken pieces. When they begin to turn white, add the garlic, ginger, and scallion. Stir-fry for about 5 minutes, or until the chicken is cooked.

3 Pour in the sauce, and when everything is well mixed, stir in the peanuts. Serve at once.

noodles & pasta

Noodles and pasta are the busy person's best friend! They are so quick to prepare—noodles often don't even need cooking and can just be soaked in boiling water for a few minutes—and they come in so many shapes and sizes that you never feel that it's 'noodles again' or 'pasta again'! For a really unusual presentation, master the art of making noodle baskets and serve filled with Chicken-Lime Salad or Chicken Chow Mein. If you'd love to try making your own pasta, try Creamy Chicken Ravioli or Chicken Tortellini—you don't need a special machine, and it's very rewarding.

Chicken with Linguine & Artichokes is a delicious option for diabetics. If you have a gluten intolerance, and have sadly concluded that your noodle- and pasta-eating days are over, don't despair—Teriyaki Chicken with Sesame Noodles uses buckwheat noodles which, in spite of their name, are not made from a type of wheat, or try Ginger Chicken with Noodles, or Pad Thai, made with rice noodles. Food manufacturers have also responded to the growing number of people with gluten intolerance and produced pastas made from ingredients such as spelt flour or rice, which can be substituted in any of the pasta recipes—follow the cooking instructions on the package, because they usually cook more quickly than wheat pasta.

teriyaki chicken with sesame noodles

ingredients

SERVES 4

4 boneless chicken breasts, about 6 oz/175 g each, with or without skin, as you wish

about 4 tbsp bottled teriyaki sauce

peanut or corn oil

cucumber fans, to garnish

sesame noodles

9 oz/250 g dried thin buckwheat noodles

1 tbsp toasted sesame oil

2 tbsp toasted sesame seeds

2 tbsp finely chopped fresh parsley

salt and pepper

method

1 Using a sharp knife, score each chicken breast diagonally across 3 times and rub all over with teriyaki sauce. Set aside to marinate for at least 10 minutes, or cover and let chill all day.

2 When you are ready to cook the chicken, preheat the broiler to high. Bring a pan of water to a boil, add the buckwheat noodles, and boil for 3 minutes, or according to the package instructions, until soft. Drain and rinse well in cold water to stop the cooking and remove excess starch, then drain again.

3 Lightly brush the broiler rack with oil. Add the chicken breasts, skin-side up, and brush again with a little extra teriyaki sauce. Broil the chicken breasts about 4 inches/10 cm from the heat, brushing occasionally with extra teriyaki sauce, for 15 minutes, or until cooked through and the juices run clear.

4 Meanwhile, heat a wok or large skillet over high heat. Add the sesame oil and heat until it shimmers. Add the noodles and stir around to heat through, then stir in the sesame seeds and parsley. Season with salt and pepper.

5 To serve, transfer the chicken breasts to plates and add a portion of noodles to each. Garnish with cucumber fans.

sweet-&-sour noodles with chicken

ingredients

SERVES 4

9 oz/250 g dried medium
    Chinese egg noodles
2 tbsp peanut or corn oil
1 onion, thinly sliced
4 boneless chicken thighs,
    skinned and cut into
    thin strips
1 carrot, peeled and cut into
    thin half-moon slices
1 red bell pepper, cored,
    seeded, and finely chopped
$3^1/2$ oz/100 g canned bamboo
    shoots (drained weight)
$2^3/4$ oz/75 g/scant $^1/2$ cup
    cashews

sweet-&-sour sauce

4 fl oz/125 ml/$^1/2$ cup water
$1^1/2$ teaspoons arrowroot
4 tbsp rice vinegar
3 tbsp brown sugar
2 tsp dark soy sauce
2 tsp tomato paste
2 large garlic cloves, very
    finely chopped
$^1/2$-inch/1-cm piece fresh
    gingerroot, peeled and
    very finely chopped
pinch of salt

method

1 Cook the noodles in a large pan of boiling water for 3 minutes, or according to the package instructions, until soft. Drain, rinse, and drain again, then set aside.

2 Meanwhile, to make the sauce, stir half of the water into the arrowroot, and set aside. Stir the remaining sauce ingredients and the remaining water together in a small pan and bring to a boil. Stir in the arrowroot mixture and continue boiling until the sauce becomes clear, glossy, and thick. Remove from the heat and set aside.

3 Heat a wok or large skillet over high heat. Add the oil and heat it until it shimmers. Add the onion and stir-fry for 1 minute. Stir in the chicken, carrot, and bell pepper and continue stir-frying for about 3 minutes, or until the chicken is cooked through.

4 Add the bamboo shoots and cashews and stir them round to brown the nuts lightly. Stir the sauce into the wok and heat until it starts to bubble. Add the noodles and use 2 forks to mix them with the chicken and vegetables. Serve immediately.

noodle basket with chicken-lime salad

ingredients

SERVES 4

peanut or corn oil, for
    deep-frying and oiling
9 oz/250 g fresh thin or
    medium Chinese egg
    noodles

chicken-lime salad

6 tbsp sour cream
6 tbsp mayonnaise
1-inch/2.5-cm piece fresh
    gingerroot, peeled and
    grated
grated rind and juice of 1 lime
4 skinless, boneless chicken
    thighs, poached and cooled,
    then cut into thin strips
1 carrot, peeled and grated
1 cucumber, cut in half
    lengthwise, seeded and
    sliced
salt and pepper
1 tbsp finely chopped fresh
    cilantro
1 tbsp finely chopped
    fresh mint
1 tbsp finely chopped fresh
    parsley
several fresh basil leaves, torn

method

1 To shape noodle baskets, you will need a special set of 2 long-handled wire baskets that clip inside each other, available from gourmet kitchen stores. Dip the larger wire basket in oil, then line it completely and evenly with one-fourth of the tangled noodles. Dip the smaller wire basket in oil, then position it inside the larger basket and clip it into position.

2 Heat 4 inches/10 cm of oil in a wok or deep-fat fryer to 350–375°F/180–190°C, or until a cube of bread browns in 30 seconds. Lower the baskets into the oil and deep-fry for 2–3 minutes, or until the noodles are golden brown. Remove the baskets from the oil and drain on paper towels. Unclip the 2 wire baskets and carefully remove the small one. Use a round-bladed knife, if necessary, to prise the noodle basket from the wire frame. Repeat to make 3 more baskets. Let the noodle baskets cool.

3 To make the salad, combine the sour cream, mayonnaise, gingerroot, and lime rind. Gradually add the lime juice until you get the flavor you like. Stir in the chicken, carrot, cucumber, salt, and pepper. Cover and let chill. Just before serving, stir in the herbs and spoon the salad into the noodle baskets.

chicken chow mein

ingredients

SERVES 4

9 oz/250 g packet medium
  egg noodles
2 tbsp sunflower oil
10 oz/280 g cooked chicken
  breasts, shredded
1 garlic clove, finely chopped
1 red bell pepper, seeded
  and thinly sliced
$3^{1}/_{2}$ oz/100 g shiitake
  mushrooms, sliced
6 scallions, sliced
$3^{1}/_{2}$ oz/100 g bean sprouts
3 tbsp soy sauce
1 tbsp sesame oil

method

1 Place the egg noodles in a large bowl or dish and break them up slightly. Pour enough boiling water over the noodles to cover and let stand while preparing the other ingredients.

2 Preheat a wok over medium heat. Add the sunflower oil and swirl it around to coat the sides of the wok. When the oil is hot, add the shredded chicken, garlic, bell pepper, mushrooms, scallions, and bean sprouts to the wok and stir-fry for about 5 minutes.

3 Drain the noodles thoroughly then add them to the wok, toss well, and stir-fry for an additional 5 minutes. Drizzle the soy sauce and sesame oil over the chow mein and toss until well combined.

4 Transfer the chicken chow mein to warmed serving bowls and serve immediately.

chicken chow mein baskets

ingredients

SERVES 4

6 tbsp water

3 tbsp soy sauce

1 tbsp cornstarch

3 tbsp peanut or corn oil

4 boneless chicken thighs,
skinned and chopped

1-inch/2.5-cm piece fresh
gingerroot, peeled and
finely chopped

2 large garlic cloves, crushed

2 celery stalks, thinly sliced

3^{1}/$_{2}$ oz/100 g white
mushrooms, wiped
and thinly sliced

4 noodle baskets made
with fresh medium
Chinese egg noodles,
to serve (see page 162)

method

1 Stir the water and soy sauce into the cornstarch in a small bowl and set aside.

2 Heat a wok or large skillet over high heat. Add 2 tablespoons of the oil and heat until it shimmers. Add the chicken and stir-fry for about 3 minutes, or until it is cooked through. Use a slotted spoon to remove the chicken from the wok.

3 Add the remaining oil to the wok, then add the gingerroot, garlic, and celery and stir-fry for 2 minutes. Add the mushrooms and continue stir-frying for an additional 2 minutes. Remove the vegetables from the wok and add them to the chicken.

4 Pour the cornstarch mixture into the wok and bring to a boil, stirring until it thickens. Return the chicken and vegetables to the wok and reheat in the sauce. Place the noodle baskets on 4 plates and divide the chicken mixture among them.

ginger chicken with noodles

ingredients

SERVES 4

2 tbsp vegetable or peanut oil

1 onion, sliced

2 garlic cloves, chopped finely

2-inch/5-cm piece fresh
   gingerroot, sliced thinly

2 carrots, sliced thinly

4 skinless, boneless chicken
   breasts, cut into cubes

10 fl oz/300 ml/1¼ cups
   chicken stock

4 tbsp Thai soy sauce

8 oz/225 g canned bamboo
   shoots, drained and rinsed

2¾ oz/75 g flat rice noodles

4 scallions, chopped, and

   4 tbsp chopped fresh
   cilantro, to garnish

method

1 Heat the oil in a wok and stir-fry the onion, garlic, gingerroot, and carrots for 1–2 minutes, until softened. Add the chicken and stir-fry for 3–4 minutes, until the chicken is cooked through and lightly browned.

2 Add the stock, soy sauce, and bamboo shoots to the wok, and gradually bring to a boil. Let simmer for 2–3 minutes. Meanwhile, soak the noodles in boiling water for 6–8 minutes. Drain well. Garnish with the scallions and cilantro and serve immediately, with the chicken stir-fry.

pad thai

ingredients

SERVES 4

8 oz/225 g rice noodles

3¼ oz/90 g peanuts, roughly chopped, plus extra, to garnish

2 tbsp lime juice

1 tbsp superfine sugar

6 tbsp Thai fish sauce

1 tsp hot chili sauce, to taste

9 oz/250 g firm bean curd (drained weight), cubed

vegetable oil, for deep-frying

3 tbsp peanut oil

1 garlic clove, crushed

1 onion, finely sliced

1 red bell pepper, seeded and thinly sliced

9 oz/250 g skinless, boneless chicken breast, cut into thin strips

3 oz/85 g bean sprouts

4½ oz/125 g snow peas

6 oz/175 g cooked shelled shrimp, cut in half lengthwise

3 eggs, beaten

lemon wedges, 4 finely chopped scallions, and 1 tbsp chopped fresh basil, to garnish

method

1 Soak the noodles in a bowl of warm water for about 20 minutes, or until soft. Drain thoroughly in a colander and set aside. Mix the peanuts, lime juice, sugar, fish sauce, and hot chili sauce together in a small bowl and set aside.

2 Rinse the bean curd in cold water, place between layers of paper towels and pat dry. Heat the oil for deep-frying in a large skillet or wok. Deep-fry the bean curd over medium heat for 2 minutes until light brown and crisp. Remove from the heat, lift the bean curd out with a slotted spoon and let drain thoroughly on paper towels.

3 Heat another large skillet or preheated wok and add the peanut oil, garlic, onion, red bell pepper, and chicken strips. Cook for 2–3 minutes. Stir in the bean sprouts and snow peas and cook for 1 minute, then add the shrimp, noodles, eggs, and bean curd and stir-fry for 4–5 minutes. Finally, add the peanut and lime juice mixture and cook for 3–4 minutes. Transfer to warmed dishes, garnish with the lemon, scallions, peanuts, and basil, and serve.

cross the bridge noodles

ingredients

SERVES 4

10$^{1}/_{2}$ oz/300 g thin egg or rice
    noodles

7 oz/200 g choi sum or
    similar green vegetable

64 fl oz/2 liters/generous
    8 cups chicken stock

$^{1}/_{2}$-inch/1-cm piece of fresh
    gingerroot, peeled

1–2 tsp salt

1 tsp sugar

1 boneless, skinless chicken
    breast, finely sliced
    diagonally

7 oz/200 g white fish fillet,
    finely sliced diagonally

1 tbsp light soy sauce

method

1 Cook the noodles according to the directions on the package. When cooked, rinse under cold water and set aside. Blanch the choi sum in a large pan of boiling water for 30 seconds. Rinse under cold water and set aside.

2 In a large pan, bring the chicken stock to a boil, then add the gingerroot, salt, and sugar and skim the surface. Add the chicken and cook for about 4 minutes, then add the fish slices and simmer for an additional 4 minutes, or until the fish and chicken are cooked through.

3 Add the noodles, choi sum and light soy sauce and bring back to a boil. Test for seasoning. Serve immediately in large individual noodle bowls.

chicken & green vegetables

ingredients

SERVES 4

9 oz/250 g dried medium Chinese egg noodles

2 tbsp peanut or corn oil

1 large garlic clove, crushed

1 fresh green chile, seeded and sliced

1 tbsp Chinese five-spice powder

2 skinless, boneless chicken breasts, cut into thin strips

2 green bell peppers, cored, seeded, and sliced

4 oz/115 g broccoli, cut into small florets

2 oz/55 g green beans, trimmed and cut into $1^1/_2$-inch/4-cm pieces

5 tbsp vegetable or chicken stock

2 tbsp bottled oyster sauce

2 tbsp soy sauce

1 tbsp rice wine or dry sherry

2 oz/55 g/$^2/_3$ cup bean sprouts

method

1 Cook the noodles in a pan of boiling water for 4 minutes, or according to the package instructions, until soft. Drain, rinse, and drain again, then set aside.

2 Heat a wok or large skillet over high heat. Add 1 tablespoon of the oil and heat until it shimmers. Add the garlic, chile, and five-spice powder and stir-fry for about 30 seconds.

3 Add the chicken and stir-fry for 3 minutes, or until it is cooked through. Use a slotted spoon to remove the chicken from the wok and set aside.

4 Add the remaining oil to the wok and heat until it shimmers. Add the bell peppers, broccoli, and beans and stir-fry for about 2 minutes. Stir in the stock, oyster sauce, soy sauce, and rice wine and return the chicken to the wok. Continue stir-frying for about 1 minute, until the chicken is reheated and the vegetables are tender, but still firm to the bite. Add the noodles and bean sprouts and use 2 forks to mix all the ingredients together.

fettuccine with chicken & onion cream sauce

ingredients

SERVES 4

1 tbsp olive oil

2 tbsp butter

1 garlic clove, chopped
very finely

4 boneless, skinless chicken
breasts

salt and pepper

1 onion, chopped finely

1 chicken bouillon cube,
crumbled

4 fl oz/125 ml/^{1}/$_2$ cup water

10 fl oz/300 ml/1^1/$_4$ cups
heavy cream

6 fl oz/175 ml/^{3}/$_4$ cup milk

6 scallions, green part
included, sliced diagonally

1^1/$_4$ oz/35 g/scant ^{1}/$_3$ cup
freshly grated Parmesan

1 lb/450 g dried fettuccine

chopped fresh flat-leaf
parsley, to garnish

method

1 Heat the oil and butter with the garlic in a large skillet over medium-low heat. Cook the garlic until just beginning to color. Add the chicken breasts and raise the heat to medium. Cook for 4–5 minutes on each side, or until the juices are no longer pink. Season with salt and pepper. Remove from the heat. Lift out the chicken breasts, leaving the oil in the skillet. Slice the breasts diagonally into thin strips and set aside.

2 Reheat the oil in the skillet. Add the onion and gently cook for 5 minutes, or until soft. Add the crumbled bouillon cube and the water. Bring to a boil, then let simmer over medium-low heat for 10 minutes. Stir in the cream, milk, scallions, and Parmesan. Let simmer until heated through and slightly thickened.

3 Cook the fettucine in boiling salted water until al dente. Drain and transfer to a warm serving dish. Layer the chicken slices over the pasta. Pour on the sauce, then garnish with parsley and serve.

tagliatelle with creamy chicken & shiitake sauce

ingredients

SERVES 4

1 oz/25 g/$^{1}/_{3}$ cup dried
   shiitake mushrooms
12 fl oz/350 ml1$^{1}/_{2}$ cups
   hot water
1 tbsp olive oil
6 bacon strips, chopped
3 boneless, skinless chicken
   breasts, sliced into strips
4 oz/115 g/2 cups fresh
   shiitake mushrooms,
   sliced
1 small onion, chopped finely
1 tsp fresh oregano or
   marjoram, chopped finely
9 fl oz/275 ml/generous 1 cup
   chicken stock
10 fl oz/300 ml/1$^{1}/_{4}$ cups
   whipping cream
salt and pepper
1 lb/450 g dried tagliatelle
2 oz/55 g/$^{1}/_{2}$ cup freshly
   grated Parmesan
chopped fresh flat-leaf
   parsley, to garnish

method

1 Put the dried mushrooms in a bowl with the hot water. Let soak for 30 minutes, or until softened. Remove, squeezing excess water back into the bowl. Strain the liquid through a fine-meshed strainer and reserve. Slice the soaked mushrooms, discarding the stems.

2 Heat the oil in a large skillet over medium heat. Add the bacon and chicken, then stir-fry for about 3 minutes. Add the dried and fresh mushrooms, onion, and oregano. Stir-fry for 5–7 minutes, or until soft. Pour in the stock and the mushroom liquid. Bring to a boil, stirring. Simmer for about 10 minutes, continuing to stir, until reduced. Add the cream and simmer for 5 minutes, stirring, until beginning to thicken. Season with salt and pepper. Remove the skillet from the heat and set aside.

3 Cook the pasta until al dente. Drain and transfer to a serving dish. Pour the sauce over the pasta. Add half the Parmesan and mix. Sprinkle with parsley and serve with the remaining Parmesan.

pasta & chicken medley

ingredients

SERVES 2

4^1/$_2$–5^1/$_2$ oz/125–150 g dried
   pasta shapes, such
   as fusilli
2 tbsp mayonnaise
2 tsp bottled pesto sauce
1 tbsp sour cream
salt and pepper
6 oz/175 g cooked skinless,
   boneless chicken
1–2 celery stalks
1 large carrot
4^1/$_2$ oz/125 g/1 cup black
   grapes (preferably
   seedless)
celery leaves, to garnish

french dressing

1 tbsp wine vinegar
3 tbsp extra virgin olive oil
salt and pepper

method

1 To make the french dressing, whisk all the ingredients together in a pitcher until smooth.

2 Bring a large, heavy-bottom pan of lightly salted water to a boil. Add the pasta, return to a boil and cook for 8–10 minutes, or until just tender but still firm to the bite. Drain thoroughly, rinse, and drain again. Transfer to a bowl and mix in 1 tablespoon of the French dressing while hot. Let stand until cold.

3 Mix the mayonnaise, pesto sauce, and sour cream together in a bowl, and season with salt and pepper. Cut the chicken into narrow strips. Cut the celery diagonally into narrow slices. Reserve a few grapes for the garnish, halve the rest, and remove any pips. Cut the carrot into julienne strips.

4 Add the chicken, celery, carrot, the halved grapes, and the mayonnaise mixture to the pasta, and toss thoroughly. Taste and adjust the seasoning, if necessary. Arrange the pasta mixture in 2 serving dishes and garnish with the reserved black grapes and the celery leaves.

pappardelle with chicken & porcini

ingredients

SERVES 4

1¹/₂ oz/40 g dried porcini
    mushrooms
6 fl oz/175 ml/³/₄ cup
    hot water
1 lb 12 oz/800 g canned
    chopped tomatoes
1 fresh red chile, seeded and
    finely chopped
3 tbsp olive oil
12 oz/350 g skinless,
    boneless chicken, cut
    into thin strips
2 garlic cloves,
    finely chopped
12 oz/350 g dried pappardelle
salt and pepper
2 tbsp chopped fresh flat-leaf
    parsley, to garnish

method

1 Place the porcini in a small bowl, add the hot water, and let soak for 30 minutes. Meanwhile, place the tomatoes and their can juices in a heavy-bottom pan and break them up with a wooden spoon, then stir in the chile. Bring to a boil, then reduce the heat and let simmer, stirring occasionally, for 30 minutes, or until reduced.

2 Remove the mushrooms from their soaking liquid with a slotted spoon, reserving the liquid. Strain the liquid into the tomatoes through a coffee filter paper, or a strainer lined with cheesecloth, and let simmer for 15 minutes.

3 Meanwhile, heat 2 tablespoons of the olive oil in a heavy-bottom skillet. Add the chicken and cook, stirring frequently, until golden brown all over and tender. Stir in the mushrooms and garlic and cook for an additional 5 minutes.

4 While the chicken is cooking, bring a large, heavy-bottom pan of lightly salted water to a boil. Add the pasta, return to a boil, and cook for 8–10 minutes, or until tender but still firm to the bite. Drain well, then transfer to a warmed serving dish. Drizzle with the remaining olive oil and toss lightly. Stir the chicken mixture into the tomato sauce, season, and spoon onto the pasta. Toss lightly, sprinkle with parsley, and serve at once.

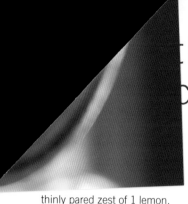

i with
chicken

thinly pared zest of 1 lemon,
    cut into julienne strips
1 tsp finely chopped fresh
    gingerroot
1 tsp sugar
salt
8 fl oz/250 ml/1 cup
    chicken stock
9 oz/250 g dried spaghetti
4 tbsp butter
8 oz/225 g skinless, boneless
    chicken breasts, diced
1 red onion, finely chopped
leaves from 2 bunches of
    flat-leaf parsley

method

1 Heat the olive oil in a heavy-bottom pan. Add the lemon zest and cook over low heat, stirring frequently, for 5 minutes. Stir in the gingerroot and sugar, season with salt, and cook, stirring constantly, for an additional 2 minutes. Pour in the chicken stock, bring to a boil, then cook for 5 minutes, or until the liquid has reduced by half.

2 Meanwhile, bring a large heavy-bottom pan of lightly salted water to a boil. Add the pasta, return to a boil, and cook for 8–10 minutes, or until tender but still firm to the bite.

3 Meanwhile, melt half the butter in a skillet. Add the chicken and onion and cook, stirring frequently, for 5 minutes, or until the chicken is light brown all over. Stir in the lemon and ginger mixture and cook for 1 minute. Stir in the parsley leaves and cook, stirring constantly, for an additional 3 minutes.

4 Drain the pasta and transfer to a warmed serving dish, then add the remaining butter and toss well. Add the chicken sauce, toss again, and serve.

pasta with chicken & feta

ingredients

SERVES 4

2 tbsp olive oil

1 lb/450 g skinless, boneless
   chicken breasts, cut into
   thin strips

6 scallions, chopped

8 oz/225 g feta cheese, diced

4 tbsp chopped fresh chives

salt and pepper

1 lb/450 g dried garganelli

tomato focaccia, to serve

method

1 Heat the olive oil in a heavy-bottom skillet. Add the chicken and cook over medium heat, stirring frequently, for 5–8 minutes, or until golden all over and cooked through. Add the scallions and cook for 2 minutes. Stir the feta cheese into the skillet with half the chives and season with salt and pepper.

2 Meanwhile, bring a large heavy-bottom pan of lightly salted water to a boil. Add the pasta, return to a boil, and cook for 8–10 minutes, or until tender but still firm to the bite. Drain well, then transfer to a warmed serving dish.

3 Spoon the chicken mixture onto the pasta, toss lightly, and serve immediately, garnished with the remaining chives and accompanied by tomato focaccia.

fruity chicken fusilli

ingredients

SERVES 4

1 lb/450 g skinless, boneless chicken, diced

1 tsp ground turmeric

1/4 tsp ground cinnamon

1/4 tsp ground cumin

1/4 tsp ground cardamom

pinch of cayenne pepper

2 tbsp peanut oil

1 onion, finely chopped

2 garlic cloves, finely chopped

12 fl oz/375 ml/1 1/2 cups chicken stock

salt

2 tbsp raisins

1 ripe mango, peeled, pitted, and diced

10 oz/280 g dried fusilli

2 tbsp chopped fresh cilantro, to garnish

method

1 Place the chicken in a shallow dish. Sprinkle with the turmeric, cinnamon, cumin, cardamom, and cayenne and toss well to coat. Cover with plastic wrap and let stand in the refrigerator for 30 minutes.

2 Heat the peanut oil in a heavy-bottom skillet. Add the onion and garlic and cook over low heat, stirring occasionally, for 5 minutes, or until softened. Add the spiced chicken and cook, stirring frequently, for 5 minutes, or until golden brown all over. Pour in the chicken stock and season with salt. Bring to a boil, add the raisins and mango, partially cover, and let simmer for 25 minutes.

3 Meanwhile, bring a large heavy-bottom pan of lightly salted water to a boil. Add the pasta, return to a boil, and cook for 8–10 minutes, or until tender but still firm to the bite. Drain and transfer to a warmed serving dish. Add the chicken mixture, toss lightly, and serve, garnished with the cilantro.

n with
& pine nut pesto

SERVES 4

2 tbsp vegetable oil

4 skinless, boneless
    chicken breasts

12 oz/350 g dried fettuccine

pepper

sprig of fresh basil, to garnish

pesto

3¹/₂ oz/100 g shredded
    fresh basil

4 fl oz/125 ml/¹/₂ cup extra-
    virgin olive oil

3 tbsp pine nuts

3 garlic cloves, minced

salt

2 oz/55 g freshly grated
    Parmesan cheese

2 tbsp freshly grated romano
    cheese

method

1 To make the pesto, place the basil, olive oil, pine nuts, garlic, and a generous pinch of salt in a food processor or blender and process until smooth. Scrape the mixture into a bowl and stir in the cheeses.

2 Heat the vegetable oil in a skillet over medium heat. Fry the chicken breasts, turning once, for 8–10 minutes until the juices are no longer pink. Cut into small cubes.

3 Cook the pasta in plenty of lightly salted boiling water until al dente. Drain and transfer to a warmed serving dish. Add the chicken and pesto, then season with pepper. Toss well to mix.

4 Garnish with a basil sprig and serve warm.

n with
ie & artichokes

SER.

4 chicken breasts, skinned

finely grated rind and juice of
   1 lemon

2 tbsp olive oil

2 garlic cloves, crushed

14 oz/400 g canned artichoke
   hearts, drained and sliced

9 oz/250 g baby plum tomatoes

10 1/2 oz/300 g dried linguine

chopped fresh parsley and
   finely grated Parmesan
   cheese, to garnish

method

1 Put each chicken breast in turn between 2 pieces of plastic wrap and bash with a rolling pin to flatten. Put the chicken into a shallow, nonmetallic dish with the lemon rind and juice and 1 tablespoon of the oil and turn to coat in the marinade. Cover and let marinate in the refrigerator for 30 minutes.

2 Heat the remaining oil in a skillet over low heat, add the garlic, and cook for 1 minute, stirring frequently. Add the artichokes and tomatoes and cook for 5 minutes, stirring occasionally. Add about half the marinade from the chicken and cook over medium heat for an additional 5 minutes.

3 Preheat the broiler to high. Remove the chicken from the remaining marinade and arrange on the broiler pan. Cook the chicken under the preheated broiler for 5 minutes each side until thoroughly cooked through. Meanwhile, add the linguine to a pan of boiling water and cook for 7–9 minutes, or until just tender.

4 Drain the pasta and return to the pan, pour over the artichoke and tomato mixture, and slice in the cooked chicken.

5 Divide among 4 warmed plates and sprinkle over the parsley and cheese.

farfalle with chicken, broccoli, & roasted red bell peppers

ingredients

SERVES 4

4 tbsp olive oil

5 tbsp butter

3 garlic cloves, chopped very finely

1 lb/450 g boneless, skinless chicken breasts, diced

$1/4$ tsp dried chili flakes

salt and pepper

1 lb/450 g small broccoli florets

$10^1/_2$ oz/300 g/$2^2/_3$ cups dried farfalle or fusilli

6 oz/175 g bottled roasted red bell peppers, drained and diced

9 fl oz/275 ml/generous 1 cup chicken stock

freshly grated Parmesan, to serve

method

1 Bring a large pan of salted water to a boil. Meanwhile, place the olive oil, butter, and garlic in a large skillet over medium-low heat. Cook the garlic until just beginning to color.

2 Add the diced chicken, then raise the heat to medium and stir-fry for 4–5 minutes, or until the chicken is no longer pink. Add the chili flakes and season with salt and pepper. Remove from the heat.

3 Plunge the broccoli into the boiling water and cook for 2 minutes, or until tender-crisp. Remove with a perforated spoon and set aside. Bring the water back to a boil. Add the pasta and cook until al dente. Drain and add to the chicken mixture in the pan. Add the broccoli and roasted bell peppers, then pour in the stock. Let simmer briskly over medium-high heat, stirring frequently, until most of the liquid has been absorbed.

4 Serve sprinkled with the Parmesan.

chicken tortellini

ingredients

SERVES 4

4 oz/115 g skinless, boneless
   chicken breast
2 oz/55 g prosciutto
1^1/$_2$ oz/40 g cooked spinach,
   well drained
1 tbsp finely
   chopped onion
2 tbsp freshly grated
   Parmesan cheese
pinch of ground allspice
1 egg, beaten
salt and pepper
double quantity pasta dough
   (see page 204)
2 tbsp chopped fresh
   flat-leaf parsley, to garnish

sauce

10 fl oz/300 ml/1^1/$_4$ cups
   light cream
2 garlic cloves, crushed
4 oz/115 g white mushrooms,
   thinly sliced
4 tbsp freshly grated
   Parmesan cheese
salt and pepper

method

1 Bring a pan of lightly salted water to a boil. Add the chicken and poach for 10 minutes. Let cool slightly, then place in a food processor with the prosciutto, spinach, and onion and process until finely chopped. Stir in the Parmesan cheese, allspice, and egg and season with salt and pepper.

2 Thinly roll out the pasta dough and cut into 1^1/$_2$–2-inch/4–5-cm circles. Place ^{1}/$_2$ teaspoon of the chicken and ham filling in the center of each circle. Fold the pieces in half and press the edges to seal, then wrap each piece around your index finger, cross over the ends, and curl the rest of the dough backward to make a navel shape. Re-roll the trimmings and repeat until all the dough is used up.

3 Bring a pan of salted water to a boil. Add the tortellini, in batches, return to a boil, and cook for 5 minutes. Drain the tortellini well and transfer to a serving dish.

4 To make the sauce, bring the cream and garlic to a boil in a small pan, then simmer for 3 minutes. Add the mushrooms and half the cheese, season with salt and pepper, and simmer for 2–3 minutes. Pour the sauce over the tortellini. Sprinkle over the remaining Parmesan cheese, garnish with the parsley, and serve.

chicken lasagna

ingredients

SERVES 6

2 tbsp olive oil

2 lb/900 g/4 cups fresh
  ground chicken

1 garlic clove, finely chopped

4 carrots, chopped

4 leeks, sliced

16 fl oz/500 ml/2 cups
  chicken stock

2 tbsp tomato paste

salt and pepper

4 oz/115 g Cheddar cheese,
  grated

1 tsp Dijon mustard

20 fl oz/625 ml/2^1/$_2$ cups hot
  béchamel sauce

4 oz/115 g dried no-precook
  lasagna

béchamel sauce

20 fl oz/625 ml/2^1/$_2$ cups milk

1 bay leaf

6 black peppercorns

2 slices of onion

mace blade

4 tbsp butter

6 tbsp all-purpose flour

salt and pepper

wild arugula and Parmesan
  shavings, to serve

method

1 To make the béchamel sauce, pour the milk into a pan and add the bay leaf, peppercorns, onion, and mace. Heat gently to just below boiling point, then remove from the heat, cover, let infuse for 10 minutes, then strain. Melt the butter in a separate pan. Sprinkle in the flour and cook over low heat, stirring constantly, for 1 minute. Gradually stir in the milk, then bring to a boil and cook, stirring, until thickened and smooth. Season.

2 Heat the oil in a heavy-bottom pan. Add the chicken and cook over medium heat, breaking it up with a wooden spoon, for 5 minutes, or until browned all over. Add the garlic, carrots, and leeks, and cook, stirring occasionally, for 5 minutes.

3 Stir in the chicken stock and tomato paste and season with salt and pepper. Bring to a boil, reduce the heat, cover, and let simmer for 30 minutes.

4 Whisk half the Cheddar cheese and the mustard into the hot béchamel sauce. In a large ovenproof dish, make alternate layers of the chicken mixture, lasagna, and cheese sauce, ending with a layer of cheese sauce. Sprinkle with the remaining Cheddar cheese and bake in a preheated oven, 375°F/190°C, for 1 hour, or until golden brown and bubbling. Serve immediately, with arugula and Parmesan shaving.

chicken cannelloni

ingredients

SERVES 4

4 skinless, boneless chicken
    breasts, diced
2 tbsp olive oil
6 tbsp butter
18 fl oz/550 ml/$2^1/_4$ cups
    heavy cream
1 tsp salt
1 tsp pepper
$^1/_4$ tsp freshly grated nutmeg
55 g/2 oz/$^1/_2$ cup freshly
    grated Parmesan cheese
1 lb/450 g ricotta cheese
1 egg, lightly beaten
1 tbsp chopped fresh oregano
2 tbsp chopped fresh basil
8 oz/225 g dried cannelloni
$2^3/_4$ oz/75 g/$^3/_4$ cup
    mozzarella cheese,
    freshly grated
fresh basil sprigs, to garnish

marinade

3 fl oz/100 ml/$^1/_3$ cup white
    wine vinegar
1 garlic clove, crushed
9 fl oz/275 ml/generous 1 cup
    olive oil

method

1 To make the marinade, mix the vinegar, garlic, and olive oil together in a large bowl. Add the chicken, cover with plastic wrap, and let marinate for 30 minutes.

2 Heat the 2 tablespoons of olive oil in a skillet. Drain the chicken and cook over medium heat for 5–7 minutes, stirring, until no longer pink. Set aside.

3 Melt the butter in a pan over medium-high heat. Add the cream, salt, pepper, and nutmeg. Stir until thickened. Reduce the heat, add the Parmesan cheese, and stir until melted. Remove from the heat.

4 Mix the ricotta, egg, and herbs together in a large bowl. Stir in the chicken. Stuff the cannelloni with the chicken mixture. Pour half the sauce into a 9 x 13-inch/23 x 33-cm baking dish. Place the stuffed cannelloni on top. Pour over the remaining sauce. Sprinkle with the mozzarella and cover with foil. Bake in a preheated oven, 350°F/180°C, for 45 minutes. Let stand for 10 minutes before serving, garnished with basil sprigs.

chicken & wild mushroom cannelloni

ingredients

SERVES 4

2 tbsp olive oil

2 garlic cloves, crushed

1 large onion, finely chopped

8 oz/225 g wild mushrooms, sliced

12 oz/350 g ground chicken

4 oz/115 g prosciutto, diced

5 fl oz/150 ml/^{2}/$_3$ cup Marsala wine

7 oz/200 g canned chopped tomatoes

1 tbsp shredded fresh basil leaves

2 tbsp tomato paste

salt and pepper

10–12 dried cannelloni tubes

butter, for greasing

20 fl oz/625 ml/2^1/$_2$ cups béchamel sauce (see page 198)

3 oz/85 g/^{3}/$_4$ cup freshly grated Parmesan cheese

method

1 Heat the olive oil in a heavy-bottom skillet. Add the garlic, onion, and mushrooms and cook over low heat, stirring frequently, for 8–10 minutes. Add the ground chicken and prosciutto and cook, stirring frequently, for 12 minutes, or until browned all over. Stir in the Marsala, tomatoes and their can juices, basil, and tomato paste and cook for 4 minutes. Season with salt and pepper, then cover and let simmer for 30 minutes. Uncover, stir, and let simmer for 15 minutes.

2 Meanwhile, bring a large, heavy-bottom pan of lightly salted water to a boil. Add the pasta, return to a boil, and cook for 8–10 minutes, or until tender but still firm to the bite. Using a slotted spoon, transfer the cannelloni tubes to a plate and pat dry with paper towels.

3 Using a teaspoon, fill the cannelloni tubes with the chicken, prosciutto, and mushroom mixture. Transfer them to a large, lightly greased ovenproof dish. Pour the béchamel sauce over them to cover completely and sprinkle with the grated Parmesan cheese.

4 Bake the cannelloni in a preheated oven, 375°F/190°C, for 30 minutes, or until golden brown and bubbling. Serve immediately.

creamy chicken ravioli

ingredients

SERVES 4

4 oz/115 g cooked skinless,
   boneless chicken breast,
   coarsely chopped
2 oz/55 g cooked spinach
2 oz/55 g prosciutto, coarsely
   chopped
1 shallot, coarsely chopped
6 tbsp freshly grated romano
   cheese
pinch of freshly grated nutmeg
2 eggs, lightly beaten
salt and pepper
1 quantity basic pasta dough
   (see below)
all-purpose flour,
   for dusting
10 fl oz/300 ml/1¹/₄ cups
   heavy cream or
   panna da cucina
2 garlic cloves,
   finely chopped
4 oz/115 g cremini
   mushrooms, thinly sliced
2 tbsp shredded fresh basil
fresh basil sprigs, to garnish

pasta dough

7 oz/200 g/1 cup all-purpose
   flour, plus extra for dusting
pinch of salt
2 eggs, lightly beaten
1 tbsp olive oil

method

1 To make the pasta dough, sift the flour into a food processor. Add the salt, eggs, and olive oil and process until the dough begins to come together. Knead on a lightly floured counter until smooth. Cover and let rest for 30 minutes.

2 Process the chicken, spinach, prosciutto, and shallot in a food processor until chopped and blended. Transfer to a bowl, stir in 2 tablespoons of the romano cheese, the nutmeg, and half the egg, and season.

3 Halve the pasta dough. Thinly roll out one half on a lightly floured counter. Cover with a dish towel and roll out the second half. Place small mounds of the filling in rows 1¹/₂ inches/ 4 cm apart on one sheet of dough and brush in between with beaten egg. Cover with the other half of dough. Press down between the mounds of filling, pushing out any air. Cut into squares and let rest on a floured dish towel for 1 hour.

4 Bring a pan of lightly salted water to a boil. Add the ravioli, in batches, return to a boil, and cook for 5 minutes. Remove and drain on paper towels, then transfer to a warmed dish.

5 Meanwhile, bring the cream to a boil with the garlic in a skillet. Let simmer for 1 minute, then add the mushrooms and 2 tablespoons of the remaining cheese. Season, then let simmer for 3 minutes. Stir in the basil, then pour the sauce over the ravioli. Sprinkle with the remaining cheese, garnish with basil sprigs, and serve.

rice

Rice dishes are popular the world over, and because different types of rice are produced in various regions, the results are also quite different.

One of the most delicious ways to eat rice is in a risotto. Rice usually needs to be left alone while it's cooking to avoid the starch being released and making the grains stick together but, for a risotto, the plump Italian Arborio rice grains are stirred constantly and explode into a glorious creaminess. Try a simple risotto topped with Chargrilled Chicken Breasts that have been marinated in an olive oil, garlic, lemon, and thyme dressing, or Chicken, Mushroom & Cashew Risotto—a delicious combination, just made to go together.

Chicken is one of the key ingredients in a Spanish paella—just the lovely name of Sunshine Paella will give your spirits a boost, before you even start eating the flavorful food! Paellas can be cooked, Spanish-style, on a barbecue grill.

Rice is consumed in vast quantities in Thailand and China. Egg-fried Rice with Chicken is a Thai classic (remember to allow several hours to let the rice cool completely), while Chicken Steamed with Rice in Lotus Leaves is a stylish Chinese dish.

And for that healthy heart, choose Jambalaya—it's good!

risotto with chargrilled chicken breast

ingredients

SERVES 4

4 boneless chicken breasts,
about 4 oz/115 g each

salt and pepper

grated rind and juice of
1 lemon

5 tbsp olive oil

1 garlic clove, crushed

8 fresh thyme sprigs,
finely chopped

3 tbsp butter

1 small onion, finely chopped

10 oz/280 g/1 1/2 cups
Arborio rice

5 fl oz/150 ml/2/3 cup
dry white wine

32 fl oz/1 liter/4 cups
simmering chicken stock

3 oz/85 g/3/4 cup freshly grated
Parmesan or
Grana Padano cheese

lemon wedges and fresh
thyme sprigs, to garnish

method

1 Place the chicken breasts in a shallow, nonmetallic dish and season. Mix together the lemon rind and juice, 4 tablespoons of the olive oil, the garlic, and thyme. Spoon over the chicken and rub in. Cover with plastic wrap and let marinate in the refrigerator for 4–6 hours, then return to room temperature.

2 Preheat a grill pan over high heat. Cook the chicken, skin-side down, for 10 minutes, or until the skin is crisp and starting to brown. Turn over and brown the underside. Reduce the heat and cook for 10–15 minutes, or until the juices run clear. Let rest on a carving board for 5 minutes, then cut into thick slices.

3 Meanwhile, melt 2 tablespoons of the butter with the remaining oil in a pan over medium heat. Cook the onion, stirring occasionally, until soft and starting to turn golden. Reduce the heat, stir in the rice, and cook, stirring, for 2–3 minutes, until translucent. Add the wine and cook, stirring, for 1 minute until reduced. Add the hot stock, a ladleful at a time, stirring constantly, until all the liquid is absorbed and the rice is creamy. Season with salt and pepper. Remove from the heat and stir in the remaining butter, then melt in the Parmesan. Serve at once, topped with the chicken slices and garnished with lemon wedges and thyme sprigs.

risotto alla milanese

ingredients

SERVES 4

4¹/₂ oz/125 g butter

2 lb/900 g skinless, boneless
   chicken breasts, thinly sliced

1 large onion, chopped

1 lb 2 oz/500 g Arborio rice

5 fl oz/150 ml white wine

1 tsp crushed saffron threads

salt and pepper

20 fl oz/625 ml/2¹/₂ cups
   simmering chicken stock

fresh flat-leaf parsley sprigs,
   to garnish

2 oz/55 g Parmesan cheese
   shavings, to serve

method

1 Melt 2 oz/55 g of the butter in a deep skillet. Add the chicken and onion and cook over medium heat, stirring occasionally, for 8–10 minutes, until golden brown.

2 Reduce the heat, add the rice and cook, stirring constantly, for a few minutes until the grains begin to swell and are thoroughly coated in the butter.

3 Add the wine and saffron and season with salt and pepper. Cook, stirring constantly, until the wine has completely evaporated. Add 2 ladlefuls of the hot stock and cook, stirring constantly, until it has been completely absorbed. Add the remaining stock, 1 ladleful at a time, stirring constantly and allowing each ladleful to be absorbed before adding the next, until all the stock has been absorbed and the rice has a creamy texture—this will take 20–25 minutes.

4 Garnish each individual plate with a parsley sprig, then serve the risotto immediately, sprinkled with the Parmesan cheese shavings and dotted with the remaining butter.

chicken, mushroom & cashew risotto

ingredients

SERVES 4

2 oz/55 g butter

1 onion, chopped

9 oz/250 g skinless, boneless
chicken breasts, diced

12 oz/350 g/1^3/$_4$ cups
Arborio rice

1 tsp ground turmeric

5 fl oz/150 ml/^{2}/$_3$ cup
white wine

46 fl oz/1.4 liters/generous
5^1/$_2$ cups simmering
chicken stock

2^3/$_4$ oz/75 g cremini
mushrooms, sliced

1^3/$_4$ oz/50 g/scant ^{1}/$_3$ cup
cashews, halved

salt and pepper

wild arugula, fresh Parmesan
cheese shavings, and
fresh basil leaves,
to garnish

method

1 Melt the butter in a large pan over medium heat. Add the onion and cook, stirring occasionally, for 5 minutes, or until softened. Add the chicken and cook, stirring frequently, for an additional 5 minutes. Reduce the heat, add the rice, and mix to coat in butter. Cook, stirring constantly, for 2–3 minutes, or until the grains are translucent. Stir in the turmeric, then add the wine. Cook, stirring constantly, for 1 minute until reduced.

2 Gradually add the hot stock, a ladleful at a time. Stir constantly and add more liquid as the rice absorbs each addition. Increase the heat to medium so that the liquid bubbles. Cook for 20 minutes, or until all the liquid is absorbed and the rice is creamy. About 3 minutes before the end of the cooking time, stir in the mushrooms and cashews. Season with salt and pepper.

3 Arrange the arugula leaves on 4 individual serving plates. Remove the risotto from the heat and spoon it over the arugula. Sprinkle over the Parmesan shavings and basil leaves and serve.

chicken risotto with saffron

ingredients

SERVES 4

4^1/$_2$ oz/125 g butter

2 lb/900 g skinless, boneless
   chicken breasts,
   thinly sliced

1 large onion, chopped

1 lb 2 oz/500 g/2^1/$_2$ cups
   Arborio rice

5 fl oz/150 ml/^{2}/$_3$ cup
   white wine

1 tsp crumbled saffron threads

46 fl oz/1.4 liters/generous
   5^1/$_2$ cups simmering
   chicken stock

salt and pepper

2 oz/55 g/^{1}/$_2$ cup freshly
   grated Parmesan cheese

method

1 Heat 2 oz/55 g of the butter in a deep pan, and add the chicken and onion and cook, stirring frequently, for 8 minutes, or until golden brown. Add the rice and mix to coat in the butter. Cook, stirring constantly for 2–3 minutes, or until the grains are translucent. Add the wine and cook, stirring constantly, for 1 minute until reduced.

2 Mix the saffron with 4 tablespoons of the hot stock. Add the liquid to the rice and cook, stirring constantly, until it is absorbed. Gradually add the remaining hot stock, a ladleful at a time. Stir constantly and add more liquid as the rice absorbs each addition. Cook for 20 minutes, or until all the liquid is absorbed and the rice is creamy. Season with salt and pepper.

3 Remove the risotto from the heat and add the remaining butter. Mix well, then stir in the Parmesan until it melts. Spoon the risotto onto warmed plates and serve at once.

sunshine paella

ingredients

SERVES 4–6

$^1/_2$ tsp saffron threads

2 tbsp hot water

5$^1/_2$ oz/150 g cod, rinsed

46 fl oz/1.4 liters/5$^1/_2$ cups
  simmering fish stock

12 large raw shrimp, shelled
  and deveined

7 oz/200 g live mussels,
  scrubbed and debearded

3 tbsp olive oil

5$^1/_2$ oz/150 g chicken breast,
  cut into bite-size chunks
  and seasoned to taste

1 large red onion, chopped

2 garlic cloves, chopped

$^1/_2$ tsp cayenne pepper

$^1/_2$ tsp paprika

8 oz/225 g tomatoes, peeled
  and cut into wedges

1 red bell pepper and
  1 yellow bell pepper,
  seeded and sliced

13 oz/375 g/generous
  1$^1/_2$ cups paella rice

salt and pepper

6 oz/175 g/scant 1 cup
  canned corn kernels,
  drained

3 hard-cooked eggs, cut into
  fourths lengthwise,
  to serve

lemon wedges, to serve

method

1 Put the saffron threads and water in a bowl and let infuse. Cook the cod in the simmering stock for 5 minutes. Rinse under cold running water, drain, cut into chunks, and set aside in a bowl. Cook the shrimp in the stock for 2 minutes. Add to the cod. Discard any mussels with broken shells or that refuse to close when tapped. Add to the stock and cook until opened. Add to the bowl with the other seafood, discarding any that remain closed.

2 Heat the oil in a paella pan over medium heat. Cook the chicken, stirring, for 5 minutes. Add the onion and cook, stirring, until softened. Add the garlic, cayenne pepper, paprika, and saffron and its soaking liquid and cook, stirring, for 1 minute. Add the tomatoes and bell peppers and cook, stirring, for 2 minutes.

3 Add the rice and cook, stirring, for 1 minute. Add most of the stock, bring to a boil, then let simmer, uncovered, for 10 minutes. Do not stir during cooking, but shake the pan once or twice and when adding ingredients. Season, then cook for 10 minutes, or until the rice is almost cooked, adding more stock if necessary. Add the seafood and corn and cook for 3 minutes.

4 When all the liquid has been absorbed and you detect a faint toasty aroma coming from the rice, remove from the heat. Cover with foil and let stand for 5 minutes. Serve topped with egg fourths and garnished with lemon wedges.

chicken & shrimp paella

ingredients

SERVES 6–8

1/2 tsp saffron threads

2 tbsp hot water

about 6 tbsp olive oil

6–8 chicken thighs, (on the
  bone, skin on), excess fat
  removed

5 oz/140 g Spanish chorizo
  sausage, casing removed,
  cut into 1/4-inch/5-mm slices

2 large onions, chopped

4 large garlic cloves, crushed

1 tsp mild or hot Spanish
  paprika, to taste

13 oz/375 g/generous
  1 1/2 cups medium-grain
  paella rice

3 1/2 oz/100 g green beans,
  chopped

3 oz/85 g/3/4 cup frozen peas

40 fl oz/1.25 liters/5 cups
  chicken stock

salt and pepper

16 live mussels, scrubbed and
  debearded (discard any
  that refuse to close)

16 raw shrimp, shelled and
  deveined

2 red bell peppers, broiled,
  peeled, seeded, and sliced

1 1/4 oz/35 g fresh parsley,
  chopped, to garnish

method

1 Put the saffron threads and water in a small bowl and let infuse for a few minutes.

2 Heat 3 tablespoons of the oil in a 12-inch/ 30-cm paella pan. Cook the chicken thighs over medium-high heat, turning frequently, for 5 minutes, or until golden and crispy. Transfer to a bowl. Add the chorizo to the pan and cook, stirring, for 1 minute, or until beginning to crisp. Add to the chicken.

3 Heat another 3 tablespoons of the oil in the pan and cook the onions, stirring frequently, for 2 minutes, then add the garlic and paprika and cook, stirring, for 3 minutes, or until the onions are soft, but not browned. Add the drained rice, beans, and peas and stir until coated in oil. Return the chicken, chorizo, and any juices to the pan. Stir in the stock and the saffron with its soaking liquid, and season with salt and pepper. Bring to a boil, stirring constantly, then let simmer, uncovered and without stirring, for 15 minutes, or until the rice is almost tender and most of the liquid has been absorbed.

4 Arrange the mussels, shrimp, and red bell pepper slices on top, then cover and let simmer, without stirring, for 5 minutes, or until the shrimp turn pink and the mussels open. Discard any mussels that remain closed. Serve immediately, sprinkled with the parsley.

chicken & duck paella with orange

ingredients

SERVES 4–6

^{1}/2 tsp saffron threads

2 tbsp hot water

6 oz/175 g skinless, boneless
   chicken breast

4 large skinless, boneless
   duck breasts

salt and pepper

2 tbsp olive oil

1 large onion, chopped

2 garlic cloves, crushed

1 tsp paprika

8 oz/225 g tomato wedges

1 orange bell pepper, broiled,
   peeled, seeded and
   chopped

6 oz/175 g canned red kidney
   beans (drained weight)

13 oz/375 g/generous
   1^1/2 cups paella rice

1 tbsp chopped fresh flat-leaf
   parsley, plus extra sprigs
   to garnish

1 tbsp freshly grated
   orange rind

2 tbsp orange juice

3^1/2 fl oz/100 ml/generous
   ^{1}/3 cup white wine

40 fl oz/1.25 liters/5 cups
   simmering chicken stock

orange wedges, to garnish

method

1 Put the saffron threads and water in a small bowl and let infuse for a few minutes.

2 Cut the chicken and duck into bite-size chunks and season. Heat the oil in a paella pan and cook the chicken and duck over medium-high heat, stirring, until golden all over. Transfer to a bowl and set aside.

3 Add the onion and cook over medium heat, stirring, until softened. Add the garlic, paprika, and saffron and its soaking liquid and cook, stirring constantly, for 1 minute. Add the tomato wedges, orange bell pepper, and beans and cook, stirring, for an additional 2 minutes.

4 Add the rice and parsley and cook, stirring, for 1 minute. Add the orange rind and juice, the wine, and most of the hot stock. Bring to a boil, then let simmer, uncovered, for 10 minutes. Do not stir during cooking, but shake the pan once or twice, and when adding ingredients. Return the chicken and duck to the pan and season. Cook for 10–15 minutes, or until the rice grains are plump and cooked, adding a little more stock if necessary.

5 When all the liquid has been absorbed and you detect a faint toasty aroma coming from the rice, remove from the heat. Cover with foil and let stand for 5 minutes. Garnish with parsley sprigs and orange wedges to serve.

paella with pork & chorizo

ingredients

SERVES 4–6

40 fl oz/1.25 liters/5 cups
  simmering fish stock
12 large raw shrimp, in their
  shells
$1/2$ tsp saffron threads
2 tbsp hot water
$3^1/2$ oz/100 g skinless,
  boneless chicken breast,
  cut into $1^1/2$-inch/
  1-cm pieces
$3^1/2$ oz/100 g pork tenderloin,
  cut into $1/2$-inch/1-cm pieces
salt and pepper
3 tbsp olive oil
$3^1/2$ oz/100 g Spanish chorizo
  sausage, casing removed,
  cut into $1/2$-inch/1-cm slices
1 large red onion, chopped
2 garlic cloves, crushed
$1/2$ tsp cayenne pepper
$1/2$ tsp paprika
1 red bell pepper, seeded
  and sliced
1 green bell pepper, seeded
  and sliced
12 cherry tomatoes, halved
13 oz/375 g/generous
  $1^1/2$ cups paella rice
1 tbsp chopped fresh parsley
2 tsp chopped fresh tarragon

method

1 Add the shrimp to the simmering stock and cook for 2 minutes, then transfer to a bowl and set aside. Put the saffron threads and water in a small bowl and let infuse.

2 Season the chicken and pork with salt and pepper. Heat the oil in a paella pan and cook the chicken, pork, and chorizo over medium heat, stirring, until golden. Add the onion and cook, stirring, until softened. Add the garlic, cayenne pepper, paprika, and saffron and its soaking liquid and cook, stirring constantly, for 1 minute. Add the bell pepper slices and tomato halves and cook, stirring, for an additional 2 minutes.

3 Add the rice and herbs and cook, stirring constantly, for 1 minute. Pour in most of the hot stock, bring to a boil, then let simmer, uncovered, for 10 minutes. Do not stir during cooking, but shake the pan once or twice and when adding ingredients. Season, then cook for an additional 10 minutes, or until the rice is almost cooked, adding a little more hot stock if necessary. Add the shrimp and cook for an additional 2 minutes.

4 When all the liquid has been absorbed and you detect a faint toasty aroma coming from the rice, remove from the heat. Cover with foil and let stand for 5 minutes. Serve.

spanish rice with chicken

ingredients

SERVES 4

3 tbsp olive oil

2 lb 12 oz/1.25 kg chicken

    pieces

salt and pepper

2 onions, sliced

6 oz/175 g/scant 1 cup

    long-grain rice

4 fl oz/125 ml/$\frac{1}{2}$ cup

    dry white wine

pinch of saffron threads,

    lightly crushed

12 fl oz/375 ml/1$\frac{1}{2}$ cups

    chicken stock

1–2 mild fresh green chiles,

    such as serrano

2 garlic cloves, finely

    chopped

2 beefsteak tomatoes, peeled,

    seeded and chopped

fresh cilantro sprigs,

    to garnish

method

1 Heat 2 tablespoons of the oil in a flameproof casserole. Season the chicken with salt and pepper, add to the casserole, and cook over medium heat, turning occasionally, for 8–10 minutes, or until golden. Transfer to a plate with a perforated spoon.

2 Add the remaining oil to the casserole. Add the onions and cook over low heat, stirring occasionally, for 5 minutes, or until translucent. Add the rice and cook, stirring, for 2 minutes, or until the grains are transparent and coated with oil.

3 Pour in the wine. Bring to a boil, then reduce the heat, cover, and let simmer for 8 minutes, or until all the liquid has been absorbed. Combine the saffron and stock and pour into the casserole. Stir in the chiles and garlic and season with salt. Cover and simmer for 15 minutes.

4 Add the tomatoes and return the chicken pieces to the casserole, pushing them down into the rice. Cover and cook for an additional 25 minutes, or until the chicken is cooked through and tender. Garnish with cilantro sprigs and serve.

greek chicken with rice

ingredients

SERVES 4

8 chicken thighs

2 tbsp corn oil

1 onion, chopped

2 garlic cloves, finely chopped

6 oz/175 g/scant 1 cup
long-grain rice

7 fl oz/225 ml/scant 1 cup
chicken stock

1 lb 12 oz/800 g canned
chopped tomatoes

1 tbsp chopped fresh thyme

2 tbsp chopped fresh oregano

12 black olives, pitted and
chopped

2 oz/55 g feta cheese,
crumbled

fresh oregano sprigs, to garnish

method

1 Remove the skin from the chicken. Heat the oil in a flameproof casserole. Add the chicken, in batches, if necessary, and cook over medium heat, turning occasionally, for 8–10 minutes, or until golden. Transfer to a plate with a perforated spoon.

2 Add the onion, garlic, long-grain rice, and 2 fl oz/50 ml/scant ¼ cup of the stock to the casserole and cook, stirring, for 5 minutes, or until the onion is softened. Pour in the remaining stock and add the tomatoes and their juices and the herbs.

3 Return the chicken thighs to the casserole, pushing them down into the rice. Bring to a boil, then reduce the heat, cover, and simmer for 25–30 minutes, or until the chicken is cooked through and tender. Stir in the olives and sprinkle the cheese on top. Garnish with oregano sprigs and serve immediately.

jambalaya

ingredients

SERVES 4

14 oz/400 g skinless, boneless
   chicken breast, diced
1 red onion, diced
1 garlic clove, crushed
20 fl oz/625 ml/2$^1/_2$ cups
   chicken stock
14 oz/400 g canned chopped
   tomatoes in tomato juice
10 oz/280 g/generous 1$^1/_2$
   cups brown rice
1–2 tsp hot chili powder
$^1/_2$ tsp paprika
1 tsp dried oregano
1 red bell pepper, seeded
   and diced
1 yellow bell pepper, seeded
   and diced
3 oz/85 g/$^1/_2$ cup frozen
   corn kernels
3 oz/85 g/$^1/_2$ cup frozen peas
3 tbsp chopped fresh parsley
pepper
crisp salad greens, to serve

method

1 Put the chicken, onion, garlic, stock, tomatoes, and rice into a large, heavy-bottom pan. Add the chili powder, paprika, and oregano and stir well. Bring to a boil, then reduce the heat, cover, and let simmer for 25 minutes.

2 Add the red and yellow bell peppers, corn, and peas to the rice mixture and return to a boil. Reduce the heat, cover, and let simmer for an additional 10 minutes, or until the rice is just tender (brown rice retains a 'nutty' texture when cooked) and most of the stock has been absorbed but is not completely dry.

3 Stir in 2 tablespoons of the parsley and season with pepper. Transfer the jambalaya to a warmed serving dish, garnish with the remaining parsley, and serve with crisp salad greens.

egg-fried rice with chicken

ingredients

SERVES 4

8 oz/225 g/generous 1 cup
  jasmine rice
3 skinless, boneless chicken
  breasts, cut into cubes
14 fl oz/400 ml/1³/₄ cups
  canned coconut milk
1³/₄ oz/50 g block creamed
  coconut, chopped
2–3 cilantro roots, chopped
thinly pared zest of 1 lemon
1 fresh green chile, seeded
  and chopped
3 fresh Thai basil leaves
1 tbsp fish sauce
1 tbsp oil
3 eggs, beaten
fresh chives and sprigs fresh
  cilantro, to garnish

method

1 Cook the rice in boiling water for 12–15 minutes, drain well, then let cool and chill overnight.

2 Put the chicken into a pan and cover with the coconut milk. Add the creamed coconut, cilantro roots, lemon zest, and chile, and bring to a boil. Let simmer for 8–10 minutes, until the chicken is tender. Remove from the heat. Stir in the basil and fish sauce.

3 Meanwhile, heat the oil in a wok and stir-fry the rice for 2–3 minutes. Pour in the eggs and stir until they have cooked and mixed with the rice. Line 4 small ovenproof bowls or ramekins with plastic wrap and pack with the rice. Turn out carefully onto serving plates and remove the plastic wrap. Garnish with long chives and sprigs of cilantro. Serve with the chicken.

hainan chicken rice

ingredients

SERVES 4–6

1 chicken, weighing
    3 lb 5 oz/1.5 kg
2 oz/55 g fresh young
    gingerroot, smashed
2 garlic cloves, smashed
1 scallion, tied in a knot
1 tsp salt
2 tbsp vegetable or peanut oil
chili or soy dipping sauce,
    to serve

rice

2 tbsp vegetable or peanut oil
5 garlic cloves, finely chopped
5 shallots, finely chopped
12 oz/350 g/scant 1³/₄ cups
    long-grain rice
30 fl oz/940 ml/3³/₄ cups
    chicken stock
1 tsp salt

method

1 Wash the chicken and dry thoroughly. Stuff the body cavity with the gingerroot, garlic, scallion, and salt.

2 In a large pan, bring enough water to a boil to submerge the chicken. Place the chicken in the pan, breast-side down. Bring the water back to a boil, then turn down the heat and simmer, covered, for 30–40 minutes. Turn the chicken over once.

3 Remove the chicken and wash in running cold water for 2 minutes to stop the cooking. Drain, then rub the oil into the skin. Set aside.

4 To prepare the rice, heat the oil in a preheated wok or deep pan. Stir-fry the garlic and shallots until fragrant. Add the rice and cook for 3 minutes, stirring rapidly. Transfer to a large pan and add the chicken stock and salt. Bring to a boil, then turn down the heat and let simmer, covered, for 20 minutes. Turn off the heat and let steam for an additional 5–10 minutes, or until the rice is perfectly cooked.

5 To serve, chop the chicken horizontally through the bone and skin into chunky wedges. Serve with the rice and a chili or soy dipping sauce.

chicken steamed with rice in lotus leaves

ingredients

SERVES 4–8

1 lb/450 g/generous 2 cups
    glutinous rice, soaked in
    cold water for 2 hours
16 fl oz/450 ml/1³/4 cups
    cold water
1 tsp salt
1 tsp vegetable or peanut oil
4 dried lotus leaves, soaked
    in hot water for 1 hour

filling

3¹/2 oz/100 g raw small
    shrimp, shelled and
    deveined
2-inch/5-cm piece of very
    fresh gingerroot
7 oz/200 g lean chicken meat,
    cut into bite-size strips
2 tsp light soy sauce
2 oz/55 g dried Chinese
    mushrooms, soaked in
    warm water for 20 minutes
1 tbsp vegetable or peanut
    oil, for frying
7 oz/200 g cha siu or pork loin
1 tbsp Shaoxing rice wine
1 tsp dark soy sauce
¹/2 tsp white pepper
1 tsp sugar

method

1 For the filling, steam the shrimp for 5 minutes and set aside. Finely grate the gingerroot, discarding the fibrous parts on the grater and reserving the liquid that drips through. Marinate the chicken in the light soy sauce and ginger juices for at least 20 minutes. Steam for a few minutes in the marinade. Set aside.

2 Drain the rice and place in a pan with the water. Bring to a boil, then add the salt and oil. Cover and cook over very low heat for 15 minutes. Divide into 8 portions and set aside.

3 Squeeze out any excess water from the mushrooms, then finely slice, discarding any tough stems. Reserve the soaking water.

4 In a preheated wok or deep pan, heat the oil and stir-fry the pork, shrimp, and mushrooms for 2 minutes. Stir in the Shaoxing, dark soy sauce, pepper, and sugar. Add the reserved mushroom soaking water, if necessary.

5 Rinse and dry the lotus leaves. Place a portion of rice in the center of each and flatten out to form a 4-inch/10-cm square. Top with the pork mixture and some pieces of chicken. Top with another portion of rice, then fold the lotus leaf to form a tight package. Steam for about 15 minutes. Let rest for 5 minutes, then serve.

chicken with vegetables & cilantro rice

ingredients

SERVES 4

2 tbsp vegetable or peanut oil

1 red onion, chopped

2 garlic cloves, chopped

1-inch/2.5-cm piece
   gingerroot, peeled and
   chopped

2 skinless, boneless chicken
   breasts, cut into strips

4 oz/115 g white mushrooms

14 oz/400 g canned
   coconut milk

2 oz/50 g sugar snap peas,
   trimmed and halved
   lengthwise

2 tbsp soy sauce

1 tbsp fish sauce

rice

1 tbsp vegetable or peanut oil

1 red onion, sliced

12 oz/350 g/3 cups rice,
   cooked and cooled

8 oz/250 g bok choy, torn into
   large pieces

handful of fresh cilantro,
   chopped

2 tbsp Thai soy sauce

method

1 Heat the oil in a wok or large skillet and sauté the onion, garlic, and gingerroot together for 1–2 minutes.

2 Add the chicken and mushrooms and cook over high heat until browned. Add the coconut milk, sugar snap peas, and sauces, and bring to a boil. Let simmer gently for 4–5 minutes until tender.

3 Heat the oil for the rice in a separate wok or large skillet and cook the onion until softened, but not browned. Add the cooked rice, bok choy, and fresh cilantro, and heat gently until the leaves have wilted and the rice is hot. Sprinkle over the soy sauce and serve immediately with the chicken.

chicken biryani

ingredients

SERVES 8

1½ tsp finely chopped fresh
   gingerroot

1½ tsp crushed fresh garlic

1 tbsp garam masala

1 tsp chili powder

½ tsp ground turmeric

2 tsp salt

5 green/white cardamom
   pods, crushed

10 fl oz/300 ml/1¼ cups
   plain yogurt

3 lb 5 oz/1.5 kg chicken,
   skinned and cut into
   8 pieces

5 fl oz/150 ml/²/₃ cup milk

1 tsp saffron strands

6 tbsp ghee

2 onions, sliced

1 lb/450 g basmati rice

2 cinnamon sticks

4 black peppercorns

1 tsp black cumin seeds

4 fresh green chiles

4 tbsp lemon juice

2–3 tbsp finely chopped fresh
   cilantro leaves

method

1 Blend the gingerroot, garlic, garam masala, chili powder, turmeric, half the salt, and the cardamoms together in a bowl. Add the yogurt and chicken pieces and mix well. Cover and let marinate in the refrigerator for 3 hours.

2 Boil the milk in a small pan, pour over the saffron, and set aside.

3 Heat the ghee in a large pan. Add the onions and cook until golden. Transfer half of the onions and ghee to a bowl and set aside.

4 Place the rice, cinnamon sticks, peppercorns, and black cumin seeds in a pan of water. Bring to a boil and remove from the heat when the rice is half-cooked. Drain and place in a bowl. Mix with the remaining salt.

5 Chop the chiles and set aside. Add the chicken mixture to the pan containing the onions. Add half each of the chopped green chiles, lemon juice, cilantro, and saffron milk. Add the rice, then the rest of the ingredients, including the reserved onions and ghee. Cover tightly and cook over low heat for 1 hour. Check that the meat is cooked through; if it is not cooked, return to the heat, and cook for an additional 15 minutes. Mix well before serving.